POW WOW country

text and photography by
Chris Roberts

American & World Geographic Publishing

*This book is dedicated to my parents, Bob and Lucy Roberts,
my son Corey, his mother Ruth Hagman,
the Wayne and Thelma Bear Medicine family and all the people on
the powwow circuit who made me welcome over the years.*

▼▼▼▼▼▼▼▼

RIGHT: *The fancy dance action of Luke Whiteman.*
FACING PAGE: *Walter Bull, Cree traditional dancer, at North American Indian Days, Browning, Montana.*
TITLE PAGE: *Rocky Boy's Reservation, Montana.*
FRONT COVER: *Boye Ladd, Winnebago fancy dancer.*
BACK COVER, LEFT: *Author Chris Roberts competing in traditional dance.*
RIGHT TOP: *Anderson Wallowing Bull, Cheyenne-Arapaho, in a traditional coyote headdress.*
CENTER: *Elk teeth decorate a Crow woman's outfit.*
BOTTOM: *The drum, in the words of one contestant, is the tool of Indian culture. Here the Kicking Woman Singers, a Blackfeet group, perform at Native American Indian Days.*

▼▼▼▼▼▼▼▼

**Library of Congress
Cataloging-in-Publication Data**

Roberts, Chris
　　Powwow country / text and photography by Chris Roberts.
　　　　p.　　cm.
　　　ISBN 1-56037-025-4
　　　1. Powwows.　I. Title.
E98.P86R62　1992
793.3'1'08997--dc20　　　　　　92-29966

▼▼▼▼▼▼▼▼

Printed in Korea.

Acknowledgments

Daryll Abrahamson
Ed Alberts
Doug Allard
Joe Arlee
Johnny Arlee
Wade Baker
Armand Bear Medicine
Durand "Smitty" Bear Medicine
Joe and Mary Bear Medicine
K.J. Bear Medicine
Wanda Bear Medicine
Wayne and Thelma Bear Medicine
Joe Begay
Clinton Bird Hat
Lionel Boyer
Virginia Brazill
Wendell Brave
Bob Brown
Tony Brown
Bobby Bull Child
Percy Bull Child
Arnold Calf Ribs
Ed Calf Robe
Ginny Cass
Gary Comes at Night
J.C. Conner
Nels Costel
Bonnie Craig
Bruce Crawford
Bob & Colleen Curfman
Dan Decker
Ervinal Denny
Phillip Dog Gun
Pat Doty Family
Jim Eagle Boy
Buster Eagle Speaker
Seymour Eagle Speaker
David E. Englund
Dean Fox
Bea Medicine Garner
Carmel Garnet
Chad Goss
Leonard Grigonis Family
Sam "Gabe" Grant
Harold Gray
Nicole Gray

Susan Gray
Mary Grounds
Bill & Theresa Hafen Family
Frank Half Moon
Wilfred Half Moon
Dennis Hanna
George Harris
Pat & Linda Hartless
Bill & Rondi Hayward
Pat Head
Louis Headley
Eugene & Barb Heavy Runner
Happy Heavy Runner
Dwight Held
Chico Her Many Horses
Randy Her Many Horses
Adrian "Crazy Horse" Holt
Anthony Johnson
Edward Johnson
Stuart J. Johnston
Butch Kathclamat
Gus Kathclamat Family
Maynard Kicking Woman Family
Pat Kennedy Family
Woody Kipp
Kuscama Dancers
Boye Ladd
Conrad & Mary Ellen LaFromboise
Richard LaFromboise
Wilson LaMere
Larry LeCounte
Lanny "Owl" Lynch
Addie Many Chief
Alex Mathews
Michelle Ducharme Matt
Bill & Doreen Meisner
Bruce Meyers
Preston Miller
Rodney Miller
Bob Mogor
Henrietta Mann Morton
Farley Mosquito
Sonny Mosquito
Leonard Mountain Chief

Norman New Rider
Adam Nordwall, Jr.
Adam Nordwall, Sr.
Walter Eugene Old Elk
Earl Old Person
Jerry Olive
Donny Parsons
Phillip & Debbie Paul Family
Linda Pease
Algae & Margaret Piapot
Jack Plumage
Stanley Pretty Paint
Garron Quill
Leon & Debbie Rattler
Joanne Rautz
Roger Reevis
Stephen "Redtail" Rickard
Lili Robbin
Peter Robbin
Richard Rock
Monte Rosebeary
Bill & Dana, Walter, Winona Runs Above
Lloyd & Margaret Runs Above
Webster & Cactus Runs Above
Ken Ryan
Marlene Salway
John Sawyer
Joe Sam & Penny Scabby Robe Family
Kenny Scabby Robe
Leroy Seth Family
Bill & Denise Sharp
Owen Slikpoo
Eva Sorrell
Alonzo Spang
Joe & Florence Standing Rock
Russell, Martin, Douglas, Kenny, Deanna Standing Rock
Dixie Starr
John Stannard
Ty Stewart
Pete & Ruby Stiffarm

Thelma Stiffarm
Videl Stump
Bob Swan
Charles Tailfeathers
Arsene Tatootsis
Merle Tendoy
John Thompson
Mark Thompson
Lloyd Top Sky
Sonny Tuttle
Dick Vick
James Watt Family
Bill Weber
James Welch
Donna Weasel Fat
Geraldine Weasel Fat
Mary Weasel Fat
Tina Weasel Fat
Dan & Ada Weasel Moccasin
Kip White Cloud Family
Lucky Whitegrass
Joe & Linda Whitehawk
Phillip Whiteman, Jr.
Phillip Whiteman, Sr.
Alvin & Darlene Windy Boy
Jonathan Windy Boy
Sam Vernon Windy Boy
Mark Wittman
Duane Wolf Black
Charlotte Wolf Child
Tony Woods, Sr., Family
Young Grey Horse Society
Gigi Sorrell Yazzie

Contents

Traditional dancer.

Introduction

The old man stood proudly at my side, his back ramrod straight, a feathered bonnet on his head. His buckskin gloved hand warmly encircled mine, its smoke-tanned odor drifted to my nose, tickling with its pungent aroma. I could barely contain my excitement yet I stood perfectly still. My parents were taking my picture with the first Indian I had ever met. He was a member of the Blood tribe, an elder. We were in Canada on our first vacation trip after emigrating to the United States from England. I was eight. It is a vivid memory that remains with me to this day. That first encounter began my interest in "things Indian." I have been involved with Indian culture ever since.

When I was sixteen, my family moved to Montana, the heart of northern Indian Country. I was active in Boy Scouts and I started an Order of the Arrow Indian Dance Team. With the intent of being authentic our troupe attended local powwows to study the costumes and dances. It was the mid-Sixties and no literature was available to provide the information we needed. Everything I found dated Indian culture to the turn of the century or before. Photographs of powwow dancers seemed limited to tourist postcards. In order to research "outfit" construction I made detailed observations and took simple 110-format pictures for many years.

In 1968 I built a "fancy dance" outfit complete with beadwork and bustles and participated in my first powwow as a dancer at the Flathead Reservation's Fourth of July Celebration in Arlee, Montana. Although dancers were curious about my interest, I was made to feel welcome and developed powwow fever. Since then I have danced Grass, Fancy and Traditional on the northern circuit. I have had the

honor of judging both singing and dancing contests as well as being chairman of Missoula's United Peoples Pow Wow in 1989.

It wasn't until 1982 that I obtained my first 35mm camera. My 110 snapshots had been popular with my subjects. I saw more than they were able to capture and I wanted to make better images of what I saw and felt. An idea came to me. Why not combine photography with my love of Indian people and culture and produce a book like I once had sought? A book that depicted the strong contemporary culture of Indian people exemplified by the powwow. A book that told the story of the powwow from a participant's point of view. A book that showed Indian people as they see themselves. My friends encouraged me to produce this book to dispel misconceptions and stereotypes.

"Not only white people, but a lot of our own people don't know what the powwow represents. There is much misconception. A lot of it created by ignorance of our customs and ways. It is taken for granted that if someone has long hair, braids, and dark skin that they know. A lot don't. That's why I support the media, photographers, writers. The powwow needs to be explained for all our benefit. As accurately as possible," said Boye Ladd, a Fancy and Exhibition dancer of the Winnebago tribe.

"There aren't any real Indians anymore. They died out about 1900. The ones today are 'Hollywood,' with their flashy feathers and Hong Kong beadwork. It's too bad they've lost their culture."

All too often comments like this are heard regarding today's Indians, many times from educated sources who, if they took the time to look carefully, would see that they are completely erroneous, misinformed and perpetuating the myth of the "dying noble Indian."

"The American Indian's way of life has always been adaptable, ongoing, continually evolving. Indian culture did go underground for a time. We weren't as open as we are now. But the sacred core remains unchanged," commented Henrietta Whiteman, a southern Cheyenne, nationally known educator and 1988 Native American Woman of the Year. "Indian culture is vital and alive. The activists' movements of the Seventies showed us it is all right to be Indian, to demonstrate our culture. In the Eighties this cultural movement grew tremendously and in the Nineties it continues to intensify. With a great sense of pride, we realize we are part of the sacred circle of life. We will endure as long as the sun and the moon and the stars."

Henri, as she prefers to be called, is voicing the sentiments of Indian people everywhere. Indian culture is alive and well and undergoing the greatest renaissance since the late 1800s. Nowhere is this growing pride and concern for traditional ways more evident than at powwows—the heartbeat of Indian Country.

This book focuses on the powwow and Indian Country. While the United States and Canada are the nations we see all around us, there is a second, less visible country, one made up of diverse languages, different customs and values, and varied peoples. It is a country of color, culture and age-old traditions. It is the country of our native peoples. They refer to it as "Indian Country," a place not limited to geographic location, but existing wherever Indian people live and work. As Indian culture continues to thrive and evolve, the powwow is at the center of its growth.

The powwow is a giant family reunion and cultural celebration. It is not a commercial event, as more money is spent than taken in. Concession stand fees, raffles and booster buttons are used to defray costs. Rarely is an admission charged on reservation powwows. They are not produced as tourist events, although visitors and spectators are welcome. Tribes host powwows to celebrate their heritage and simply to enjoy being Indian.

A Sioux drum group at North American Indian Days.

Indian people dance and sing year-round. From Memorial Day (last Monday in May) until Labor Day (first Monday in September) is the primary season when families travel to the big powwows, setting up their vans, tents and tipis, sometimes in the exact spot at which they have camped for years. Observers and participants alike will be expected to respect the customs and traditions of the hosting tribe. Powwow people are friendly. They are interested in those who are interested in them. They go out of their way to make visitors welcome. The editor of Canada's leading Indian magazine, *Wind-speaker,* said, "The 'gathering' aspect of powwows is significant. Time and again dancers and spectators tell us that things they like best about dancing or visiting at powwows is the people they meet and the friends they make. Powwows break down the barriers and unify all who take part. Whether you're from the southernmost regions of the United States or far northern Canada—common ground is found at a powwow.

"Today the celebration aspect of powwows is as important as a hundred years ago when the dancers celebrated a successful hunt or a victorious war party. But now, the celebration is of being Indian. Of having a unique culture and long reaching history. Of letting the spirit fly with the beat of the drum."

You could fly to many exotic places of the world and not discover a celebration as rich as the one that exists in North America's own backyard.

I have written and photographed this book at the urging of powwow people. They feel it is important to preserve a time and place, depict the pride and richness of Indian people, and capture the color and celebration of North America's oldest indigenous social and cultural event. In the early 1980s I made a committed effort to reflect Indian dignity and spirit. The results are the photographs in this book, which were made in Montana on the Blackfeet, Rocky Boy, Flathead, and Crow reservations. Due however to the universal nature of powwows they accurately reflect the northern plains circuit. The participants are from all over the western U.S. and Canada; many who call the southern circuit their home were traveling "up north."

I photograph with a 35mm camera, zoom lenses and a favorite 55mm macro lens that gives sharp detail for close-up portraits. I use Kodachrome 25 or Fujichrome 50 film. For the text, I have tried to remember conversations and shared discussions with participants and spectators, about the pleasures of the powwow. The words in this book are the words and information of the many friends and acquaintances I have made over the years.

Almost thirty-five years have passed since that proud Blood elder consented to pose for a picture with an excited little boy. That little boy is now a man with a little boy of his own. The old man, that gentle spirit, has joined the Creator. His spirit lives on and is not forgotten. I ask his blessing for the people who live in Indian Country.

Dusk arrives on the northern Montana plains. A gentle curtain descends upon the rolling land as the wind from the west dies. The sun paints a magenta hue on the eastern slope of the snow-capped Rocky Mountains. Clouds turn orange and deepen to red. It's a Charlie Russell sky. The encampment bustles with evening activity, a smoky haze from cooking fires drifts around painted Blackfeet tipis. Horses are tethered, children play and dogs bark. The Bear Medicine family is sharing food with visitors. Phillip Dog Gun is donning his dance outfit. Boye Ladd is resting up for the fancy dance finals and Joe Sam Scabby Robe rounds up his kids. A public address system whistles and squawks as it warms up.

"A Ho! All you dancers start getting ready. Grand Entry in ten minutes!" Earl Old Person calls for the participants to make their way to the arbor. The Kicking Woman Singers' steady drumbeat and northern plains flag song carries through the cooling air: "As long as the flag shall wave, Indian people shall live."

My feet move with anticipation as I make the final adjustments on my dance outfit. The spirit of the drum starts to move me and my heart quickens. I emerge from my "lodge," dance bells ringing, bustle feathers fluttering in the breeze. Picking up my last piece of equipment, my camera with lenses and film, I am ready to compete as a Traditional dancer on the powwow circuit. I ask the Creator to help my photographic images bring forth the richness and strength of Indian culture and to show the pride and love of life that so characterizes The People.

All the people who touched my life, taught me, shared with me, welcomed me and encouraged me on the powwow trail—this book is for you.

Byron Heavy Runner applies his paint at Elmo's Standing Arrow Powwow on the Flathead Indian Reservation, Montana.

Jaycene Windy Boy chooses a quilt to present to a recipient at the Windy Boy Family giveaway.

History of the Powwow

▼▼▼▼▼▼▼▼▼▼▼▼▼

Exactly when the modern-day powwow began is difficult to pinpoint. It certainly can be traced for a hundred years, through definite developmental periods. Today the powwow continually expands in scope and popularity.

The powwow is not limited to dancing and singing "Indian," but is an overall term given to a gathering of Indian people in a social event. With dancing as its primary focus, the powwow is a celebration of culture. Besides the "intertribal" dancing, many other events are scheduled into the four- to five-day period over which a powwow takes place. Indian people gather to rodeo, gamble at hand games, honor relatives with giveaways, compete in athletic runs and horse races, parade, schedule exhibition events and special ceremonies, feed friends and visitors, and buy a great variety of goods at concession stands. Visiting with friends and acquaintances, however, commands the prime attraction of all participants.

Early History

According to Boye Ladd, champion Winnebago fancy dancer and historian, "Songs and dances evolved around the imitation of animals and natural forces and were held sacred." The word powwow derives from the Algonquian for a gathering of medicine men and spiritual leaders in a curing ceremony, a "pauau" or "pau wau." When early European explorers observed these religious events, with the accompanying dances, they mispronounced the name as powwow and believed it referred to any

large gathering of Indian people. The term spread, and, as Indian tribes learned English, they accepted the definition given to their gatherings.

The Algonquian word "pauau" or "pau wau," has been Anglicized into the word powwow, which also has become a pan-Indian term. The English language has adopted many other words of Indian origin, most notable of which are twenty-five state names. Place names are but an example of American Indian contributions to the language and rich cultural life of the United States. A powwow is an outgrowth of the religious and social dances of the plains tribes, it is a celebration of culture with dancing as its primary focus.

Henrietta Mann Morton
Educator
Southern Cheyenne

Historically, tribes in North America held ceremonies celebrating successful hunts, food gathering, or warfare. These ceremonies allowed the people to give thanks, honor their deceased relatives, or deal with special honors such as name-giving ceremonies, adoptions and coming of age rites. Many times they were held to renew allegiances and maintain friendships with members of visiting tribes. The ceremonies often involved dancing and feasting.

Indian people depended on the land for their food, clothing and shelter. If they stayed in large bands, they overly taxed "Mother Earth," so they split into smaller family groups. During the winter, when activity was limited, they had time to decorate special clothing for the summer's reunion.

There is an old story that says that at one time all Indian people were in harmony with nature. They spoke the same language. It is said that our ceremonies, songs and dances are derivatives and interpretations of what we learned from nature. We were able to speak with animals and learn from them. We still hold that tie today. This is where we get those animal behavioral type dances that are part of our sacred ways. Even in the powwow there is an open line, a connection between man and nature.

Boye Ladd
Fancy and Exhibition Dancer
Winnebago

These summer reunions took place at prearranged locations and dates. All tribal members gathered for social activities and religious ceremonies that reaffirmed their unity, and clans and societies held their annual rites. Cultural traditions strengthened with these gatherings. Today's powwow grew out of these religious and social dances of the plains tribes.

The history of the powwow as I learned it comes through my family from generation to generation. Our people would all come together once or twice a year for a celebration. There would be a big gathering of family and friends. Barterers would come to trade and sell. There would be horse races and skill contests and at night everyone would dance. Families would host feasts and giveaways. All of this still goes on today. We teach our children that this coming together is good. Wherever I go, I see Indian people being thanked for traveling to the powwow, camping out and visiting for days at a time.

Joe Sam Scabby Robe
Fancy and Exhibition Dancer
Blackfeet

The Beginnings—Grass Dance

The powwow dance goes back to the Omaha to a period about four hundred years ago. Today there are a lot of societies, especially in the Dakotas, who still refer to the "Omaha dances." Down in Oklahoma there are societies evolved around warriors. The Hethuska societies, the stealthtakers. The Red Feather societies, the Kit Fox, the Dog Soldiers, all these societies evolve around warriors and what they have done in battle. Eagle feathers worn in these societies indicate coup that has been counted by brave deeds in battle. These ways still affect the powwow.

An old story that goes back to a great-great-great-grandfather says that powwow dancing originated from four Omaha brothers who were warriors. They had returned from an expedition and performed a war dance in celebration of their success. This was way before the coming of the white man. They were not necessarily celebrating the taking of a life but pride in their good medicine. The dance they performed was a celebration of their good fortune as members of a family, a society, a clan, and a tribe. It was a dance based in pride. We still see that pride today.

George P. Horse Capture
Curator, Buffalo Bill Historical Center
Gros Ventre

Boye Ladd

Plains Indian dancing was of three basic varieties: dream-cult dancing like the ill-fated Ghost Dance, vow fulfillment dances like the Sundance, and warrior society dancing. Contemporary powwow dancing is generally credited to the Hethuska (war dance) Societies of the Oklahoma Ponca, and the Omaha and Pawnee's "grass" dance. These two Nebraska tribes danced first with scalps attached to their belts and then switched to braided sweetgrass, which was representative of those scalps, when the government discouraged intertribal warfare. The Pawnee gave the dance to the Omaha, who in turn gave the dance to the Sioux in the early 1870s.

It is said that the initial traditional Grass Dance outfit came from the Hethuska society of the Omaha tribe and slowly spread northward. A Lakota friend and dancer from Wounded Knee, Mike Her Many Horses, states that his grandfather Ben Marrowbone said that in the mid-1870s a woman from Spotted Tail's band of Rosebud Sioux married an Omaha man and the Omaha people gave this dance to them as a wedding gift. From the Sioux it traveled to the Assiniboine, then to the Gros Ventre, and then the Blackfeet.

The Sioux helped spread it to other tribes. In the Sioux version of the "Omaha dance," society members danced a depiction of scouting, scalping, and killing an enemy. When the Indian wars ended, the warrior societies declined but the "Omaha grass dance" continued. It became a social show dance in which the dancer concentrated on intricate body and head movements, keeping his headdress feathers in constant motion.

Government Repression

From the time of the Indian Wars in the late 1800s, both the U.S. and Canadian governments were afraid of Indian unity and did all they could to repress native culture and traditions. Indian people were rounded up and placed on reservations and restricted in their movements. They could not leave reservations without permission. Sitting Bull was tracked down and defeated in both body and spirit.

The Ghost Dance religion sprang up only to die a real and painful death at Wounded Knee, South Dakota. Indian language, culture and traditions were encouraged to die along with Big Foot and his band. In the 1890s, Indian dances and traditional ceremonies such as the Sundance were strictly forbidden. Braids were not allowed. Children sent to boarding schools to learn the whiteman's ways were never seen again. Land was usurped and opened for white settlement. Food rations were "appropriated" and blankets infected with smallpox to ensure that the people would die along with their culture.

It was a shameful period. As time went on, government attitudes began to change, but even as late as the 1920s native culture and social events were frowned upon. The following excerpt from a U.S. Department of Interior circular to all reservation superintendents regarding dancing illustrates this well. Circular No. 1665, April 26, 1921 stated that:

"The latest reports of Superintendents on the subject of Indian dances reveals encouraging conditions, indicating they are growing less frequent, are of shorter duration, and interfere less with the Indian's domestic affairs, and have fewer barbaric features....the native dance still has enough evil tendencies to furnish a retarding influence and a troublesome situation...the dance is apt to be harmful and we should control it by educational processes as far as possible, but if necessary by punitive measures. I regard such restriction as applicable to any dance which involves...self torture, immoral relations between the sexes, sacrificial destruction of useful articles, the reckless giving away of property, and frequent or prolonged periods of celebration which brings Indians together from remote points to the neglect of their crops, livestock and home interests...these suggestions are offered with a view

Traditional dancers lined up after the grand entry at Browning.

I don't think it is right to use weak drums for big dance contests. Why put up a thousand or fifteen hundred dollars for a contest and not give the dancers good music? They deserve to be able to show their best style. It just burns and wastes energy trying to dance to the poorer groups. Let them earn the right to sing contest songs by improving their music. People came to see a good show. Give them good music, you'll see a great show.

Boye Ladd, Fancy Dancer
Winnebago

towards a better control of Indian dancing so far as it retains elements of savagery and demoralizing practices."

Respectfully,
Chas. H. Burke
Commissioner

Emergence

Following non-Indian contact, the powwow, like many other of our dances, was misunderstood and subject to repression by the United States Federal Government. Powwows, however, have endured; so have the people, as have many other aspects of their culture. Just as important, so has the Indian spirit.
Henrietta Mann Morton

By the late 1930s, bureaucratic influences and residential/mission schools nearly wiped out Indian lifestyles, language, customs and religion. Fortunately the government wasn't successful in eliminating either religious or social dances. The Wild West shows of the early 20th century employed Indians to add excitement to their productions. The performers were encouraged to dance fancier. This influence may have started "fancy dance," although that theory can't be verified.

The grass dance is a dance that goes back to the beginning of the origins of powwow. The Omahas used sweet grass braids as a fringe on their dance clothes. It is said that these represented scalps. Then the Omahas started using feathers as decorations. They had feathered arm bustles, knee bustles, back bustles, and big feathered headdresses. This became known as the Omaha dance and then fancy dance.
Boye Ladd

Oklahoma tribes were at the center of the powwow emergence. The Ponca Fair and Pow Wow originated in 1877. The dances lasted four days and attracted people from over 100 miles away. They traveled by foot, horseback and wagon. Nineteen-sixteen saw the beginnings of the Anadarko Fair.

In 1925, the Haskell Institute in Lawrence, Kansas held a dance contest to determine the world's championship. The old Omaha grass dance became fancied up with colorful feathered bustles, and fancy dancing was born. Indian people have always borrowed from each other and the new style of costuming and dancing quickly spread to other plains tribes.

Rejuvenation

Attitudes started changing in the late 1940s and early 1950s. World War II was over and many Indians were veteran "warriors." Clans and societies welcomed these patriots. Powwows were initiated to honor the veterans, a practice that continues to this day.

The modern-day powwow can be traced to the Grass Dance societies that formed around the turn of the century. The Grass Dance is known by many different names among various tribes and has an interesting history. It can be traced back to the war dances and victory celebrations of an earlier era. Originally only experienced warriors could belong to Grass Dance societies.
Jonathan Windy Boy
Grass Dancer
Chippewa-Cree

Indian people look to their culture for strength and identity. This cultural awareness intensified during the 1960s civil rights movement, when Indian people took a renewed pride in being

The Eagle Whistles Drum Group at Helena's
Big Sky Pow Wow.

Indian. Today's proliferation of powwows is the strongest evidence of this cultural rejuvenation.

"The contemporary powwow acts as a catalyst to bring former tribal enemies together in a social setting. Tribal wars are limited to the intense competition in the arena," Woody Kipp pointed out. "White society dances are categorized according to age groups. Indian dances include the very oldest to the very youngest. Entire extended families join in."

Back in the Fifties there was still a lot of animosity between tribes. You wouldn't see Crows and Cheyennes or Crows and Sioux sitting at the same drum, let alone being at the same powwow. Today intertribalism is very much alive. The modern-day powwow has brought a lot of tribes together, it's brought unity. We are saying "we" now as opposed to saying only "Sioux," "Cheyenne," or "Crow."

Boye Ladd

Powwows were always with us. They were a way of celebrating our lives as Indians. As our land shrunk and we were put on reservations, intertribal warfare ceased and powwows became a way for us to still compete with each other. We could trade, feast, giveaway, and dance. We had a new way of demonstrating our pride without stealing horses or taking lives.

Phillip Paul
Traditional Dancer
Flathead

Maggie Black Kettle, a Canadian Blood, is somewhere in her 70s. She is an honored presence at many Northwest powwows, where she proudly watches the young girls compete in the fancy shawl category. Her bright, sparkling eyes follow every step and movement. While attending Missoula, Montana's Kyi Yo Pow Wow she commented, "We never had powwows when I was young. They were forbidden as 'devil's work.' I attended my first powwow in the 1940s. Now I make all my own dresses for dancing. My children and grandchildren dance. It is part of our way of life. The powwow will never die out; it is so popular. All the young people dance and meet friends. I go, too. I meet new people and old friends."

Traditionally a powwow celebration was expressed through song and dance. However, a significant and often forgotten part of these get-togethers was the exchange of gifts. This practice was an important part of reestablishing old ties and friendships with each other. When a gift was given, proper etiquette required that a gift be given in return. Throughout the years the powwow has evolved into a tradition exemplifying generosity and giving.

Jonathan Windy Boy

Anjo Scabby Robe is seven. He wears a baseball cap from which protrude three braids in the traditional Blackfeet way. He has been a champion dancer since he was three. His dad, Joe Sam, his younger sister, Sammy Jo, and mom, Penny, also dance. He understands Blackfeet and "sings Indian." Uncle Kenneth's popular Black Lodge Singers' newest dance song moves Anjo's feet as he dresses in his grass dance outfit. He is a kaleidoscope of colors—red, yellow, green, white, and blue—fringe, feathers, and brilliant beadwork.

Confident and proud before competing in the Junior Boys Contest at North American Indian Days in Browning, Montana, Anjo says, "I always dance good. Sometimes I dance better and win money. Some of it I save, some of it I use to buy toys and

candy, and sometimes I just give it to my mom." Anjo has never known a world without powwows and Anjo never will.

The Annual Red Bottom Celebration at Fraser, Montana is one of the oldest, longest-running Indian celebrations on the northern great plains. It had its beginning in 1903. The late Walter Clark, Jr. lay seriously ill. There were no medical facilities available and transportation was by foot or horse team and wagon. Walter's father made a vow in the age-old tradition of the Assiniboine Indians. If his son lived he would sponsor a feast, a large giveaway, and a dance. Walter Clark, Sr. was a man of great wealth. It is told that he gave away horses, teams of wagons, buggies, live beef, and that he slaughtered many cows to feed the relatives and friends who came to celebrate his son's return to health. Thus was born the annual event we carry on today.
Robert Four Star, Tribal Elder
Assiniboine

Regardless of where we live, whether it is in an urban setting or on a reservation, or whether the event is a major encampment or a mini-powwow, we continue to express our cultures in the powwow. For a brief period of time we can put aside our professional non-Indian roles and come together from our di-

verse tribal backgrounds and with a unity of spirit enjoy the dance and celebrate life.
Henrietta Mann Morton

The powwow also serves to establish and increase individual or tribal social status. Well organized, hospitable celebrations, with good singers and dancers, bring honors and accolades to tribes, sponsoring organizations or families. The "moccasin telegraph" buzzes with comments like "Boy, they run a good Indian days," or "They treat you good over there." The following years attendance increases and the particular event obtains a "must attend" status, achieving honor and increased respect.

If you are the host, let the visitors have the money and prizes. In this way you show your pride in living. Make sure they have good water and facilities. Invite them to your camp for food and rest. Treat them like you want to be treated. Show them what it means to be Indian.

Phillip Paul

The powwow brings people together in a common purpose. Families interact among themselves and other families. Tribal members reaffirm their heritage and identity. Hands of friendship extend to other tribes and cultures. A network of support strengthens an entire race of people. To be Indian is to be proud, to know who you are, where you came from. Knowing these things helps Indian people to guide their future. The interaction of families with their children and their elders insures a continuation of culture. The powwow provides forum in which this can take place.

The Powwow Circuit

▼▼▼▼▼▼▼▼▼▼▼▼▼▼▼▼▼

"Good Morning, Indian America! Roll over, you sleepy Indians, let's shake a few feathers," boomed the voice over the public address system. Reenacting the tradition of camp crier, Russell Standing Rock, the powwow announcer, awoke the camp with his characteristic good humor. He announced the day's scheduled events as the camp slowly stirred and weary dancers stretched. "Come on, the sun is up, time to fix coffee, have breakfast ready, I'm coming to visit my friends," he exhorted, "and I'm hungry."

I had awakened with the sun to photograph the camp and its tipis lit by the early morning sky. I was stiff from dancing late into the cool Montana night and tired from yesterday's long drive.

My family and I had arrived the previous day while twilight was casting its golden glow. Buckskin fringes swayed and bustle feathers fluttered in the cooling breeze of a northern plains evening, as dancers spun and twisted their way into the bough-bedecked arbor. The Grand Entry was under way. We had traveled many hot Montana miles to visit our friends and participate in Rocky Boy's Reservation Memorial Pow Wow. Cresting a hill we were surprised by the size of the encampment. A haze of smoke and dust hung over the 3,000 people attending this annual event. Tipis, tents, trucks, cars and campers were jammed together everywhere.

As we circled the camp, my old Cree friend, Kenneth Standing Rock, pointed out a space next to his family's camping spot. We pulled in next to a brilliant yellow van with "Navaho Country" license

The back bustle of John Grounds, a Blackfeet, reveals elaborate craftsmanship.

Money has created an increased interest in powwows. With money comes jealousy. Jealousy exists towards one another too much. A lot of people don't value friendships like they used to. Long ago we used to give our best and give a lot. Now that is not so. Dance outfits are judged too much for their quality and the judges don't always see the dancing ability. If we go back to the old way it will be our "tiny tots" who make the change.

Kip White Cloud, Traditional Dancer
Sioux

plates. The van's sides were adorned with a painting of a war bonneted warrior. After our camp was made, we prepared to join the 1,500 costumed dancers in the circular arbor at the camp's center.

For about twenty-five years, "Powwow Fever" has affected me, and is an integral part of my summers. I am a non-Indian participant, born in London and reared in Missoula, Montana. My fascination with Indian ways and powwow celebrations began when I was a young boy. Through the years, friendships with Indian peers and a strong interest in native cultures and traditions have intensified my involvement in the powwow circuit, first as a dancer, and now as a photographer and writer.

I attend powwows for numerous reasons, including an eagerness to rekindle old acquaintances and gain new friendships. I photograph the gatherings and activities to preserve a time and place, and to capture the color and pageantry of the celebration of "being Indian." I write to evoke the feelings and experiences encountered at a powwow, to bring forth the essence of the powwow spirit.

One should know what a powwow is before it can be felt or understood. There is an extreme shortage of literature on the powwow and what is written is usually centered on a specific powwow or region. I hope that this book will provide a general understanding of the overall event, and both the Southern and Northern styles that can be observed in the United States and Canada. Throughout this book I will use words of the people who are actively involved in powwow life to help tell the story.

A common mistake by observers is to limit their definition of a powwow to only dance-oriented activities. The powwow is more than that. The term encompasses the entire celebration that takes place over a period of many days. Powwows that are just dance oriented and last for an evening are usually referred to as "dances."

There is no single word that describes the powwow. Powwow is Indian. Though nowadays there is an emphasis on contest dancing, it is still the same as when I grew up. The powwow is a place of healing, praying, dancing and singing. A place to join others in pride and respect. A place to feel good. Powwow means the gathering of relations, of people. A place people come to get well, feel good about themselves, about their people. It is a place of good spirits. When you're feeling sad, come to a powwow and you'll be happy again. There will be a feeling you didn't have when you first came there.

Tony Brown
Fancy Dancer–Hoop Dancer
Oneida-Sioux-Flathead

The powwow is a giant family reunion and a cultural celebration whose attendance often doubles a reservation's population. Concession stands, raffles, bingo, and booster button sales help defray the costs. Rarely is an admission fee charged.

Tribes, organizations, family groups and even academic institutions, host or sponsor powwows for a variety of reasons. There are five basic categories, some of which overlap: holiday, honoring, memorial, benefit, and large annual commercial powwows.

Smaller local benefit powwows help generate funds in the "off season" to produce the larger summer events. Family- or organization-sponsored powwows serve as fund-raisers for a variety of causes. The money generated by the sale of raffle tickets, concessions, and blanket dances may be used to build scholarship funds, help a needy family, or finance a large giveaway.

The southern powwow circuit, centered in Oklahoma, hosts more of the honoring and benefit powwows. The northern circuit seems to favor holiday and large commercial events.

Indian dancers are like professional rodeo cowboys. They both travel a circuit, both wear numbers when they compete, both have to be in shape, to train. The outcome of both contests are unpredictable. Cowboys depend on the steer and the horses, dancers on whether they get good drums or judges.

Kip White Cloud, Traditional Dancer
Sioux

Junior Two Teeth, a Cree, dances traditional in a Mandan-style eagle feather headdress.

Honoring powwows are held to honor a returning or retiring veteran, or a person well known for community service. A family may host an honoring powwow to celebrate a person's birthday or anniversary.

Memorial powwows commemorate the deceased, or a particular event, such as the establishment of the reservation. In Oklahoma this form of powwow may mark the end of a one-year mourning period and involve a large giveaway of blankets, food, and cash.

One of the most common powwows in Oklahoma is the benefit. These are held to raise money for various tribal organizations or to aid families or individuals. They are also used to raise money for the large annual powwow.

Holidays are a good reason to host a powwow. There are many Memorial Day, Fourth of July, Labor Day, Thanksgiving and Christmas Indian celebrations. The Annual Pawnee Homecoming Pow Wow held in Oklahoma over July 4th has an emphasis on veterans, as well as being a large commercial event.

North American Indian Days, hosted by the Blackfeet tribe in Browning, Montana, on the second weekend in July, is a prime example of a large commercial annual powwow. Located only twelve miles from Glacier National Park, it attracts large crowds of Indian and non-Indian visitors. In 1990 the dance contest purse of $23,000 drew hundreds of dancers from all areas of the country.

Powwows can be indoor events like the University of Montana's Kyi Yo Pow Wow or they can be outdoor events with massive campgrounds and hundreds of tipis like Crow Fair, which bills itself as "Tipi Capital of the World."

It is the large outdoor annual powwow, taking place over a three- to four-day period, on which this book primarily focuses. These powwows almost always take place on the same weekend every year

For me, it's a spiritual thing. I come to a powwow to be an Indian, to get a sense of myself, a sense of pride and heritage. This is part of Indian spirituality, to help each other and to celebrate with each other. When I come to powwows I gain strength to carry on with the endeavors of my life.

Rachel Snow, Fancy Shawl Dancer
Stoney

Color is everywhere in the details of outfits and the materials for making them.

 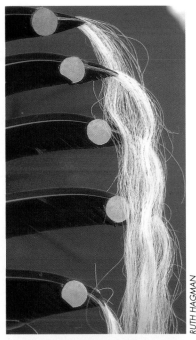

RUTH HAGMAN

and are part of a circuit through which dancers, singers, and their families travel to year after year.

Powwows take place within circuits similar to leagues in athletic sports. But unlike those leagues, formal recognition of these circuits does not exist. The circuit traveled by dancers and their families depends in part on their personal whims, money and time available, and friends they wish to encounter. It is interesting to note that these circuits also correspond to what anthropologists refer to as "cultural areas." Circuits exist in the coastal, plateau, great basin, mountain, plains, woodland, eastern, southern, and south-western tribal areas. Distinct stylistic differences separate the northern plains-influenced circuits from the southern ones, but participants travel as they wish, without tribal restrictions or limitations.

Powwows take place in geographic circuits which are roughly a half day's drive in diameter. These circuits overlap. I've been able to identify about sixteen in the U.S. and Canada. The two primary circuits are the Northern and Southern. The more formal southern plains influence is centered in Oklahoma and the looser Northern style is centered in the Dakotas, Montana, and the Canadian provinces of Alberta and Saskatchewan.

Boye Ladd
Fancy and Exhibition Dancer
Winnebago

Dates for powwows are selected so as not to conflict with other events within the immediate circuit. Once a date is established sponsors do not change that date without risking confusion or a major drop in attendance. On the southern circuit most of the powwows occur during the pleasant months of spring. High temperatures and uncomfortable weather in summer contribute to a downturn in the number of powwows sponsored. Not so in cooler northern climes; summer sees powwow season in full swing.

Powwows are promoted primarily through word of mouth. Sponsors print posters and mailers to nudge the word along. Contestants who registered the previous year at a particular event will receive a mailer the next year. Posters, displaying photographs of head dancers, princesses and host drums, list the cash prizes offered. Committee members tack them in visible locations and distribute them by hand to singers, dancers and spectators. Emcees constantly announce dates day and night. Word travels the "moccasin telegraph" faster and more effectively than on any other medium.

The powwow circuit is a large family. Powwow country is tied into the family. If someone is in need the people share with them, money for gas to make it home, a place to sleep, or food to eat. I can travel a great distance and be treated like I was at home. Whether it be Arizona or northern Canada, from Alberta to Ontario, people treat me like their own.

Kip White Cloud
Traditional Dancer
Sioux

Families traveling through circuits receive hospitality from host tribes. Some people travel for months at a time, staying with friends or in motels between powwows. Moving from weekend to weekend, they cover hundreds of miles. Plains tribes followed the buffalo and were historically nomadic. Contemporary circuit followers repeat that cultural trait. Large families who sing and dance can subsist on contest winnings and "drum money" paid out for their singing.

For Indians to dance professionally is not bad. It is another way of life. We have money powwows and non-money powwows. It is nice to be able to choose. For many powwow participants, money is necessary to put food on the table and a roof over their children's heads. If money is generated every weekend, then the dance can become a profession. There is a dilemma I feel sad about. Many champions are well respected in powwow circles, but come Monday they are a janitor for the white man. Outside of powwow circles they are looked down upon. If there is more money available this way of life becomes a respected profession. After all if the white can go and hit a ball with a stick for a million dollars, why can't the Indian earn a living at his "sport"?

Boye Ladd

BELOW: A teen fancy shawl dancer competes at North American Indian Days.
FACING PAGE: The bead- and feather-work of an arm bustle.

Hackle feather bustles of Oklahoma-style fancy dancers at Rocky Boy, Montana.

Everywhere they go they meet new people, adding them to mental friendship lists. Many times they see the same faces from weekend to weekend until they reach new and distant lands. As they wander from circuit to circuit, fellow travelers become hosts on their homelands. In turn, the wandering family will host friends who come to their own reservation. Hosts become visitors, and visitors hosts. These two categories are the primary forms of social structure at powwows. "Come visit us at Indian days. We will put up a tipi for you, butcher a beef, make you welcome," are frequent parting words.

Powwows are a celebration of life. We dance, sing, and gather to be happy that we are alive. Happy that we can still see, eat, walk, run, and enjoy family and friends that have gathered for this celebration. The opening of the powwow is a prayer that we will learn from and share with one another. Our dance outfits are made to reflect the wearer's personality. Our songs are sung to show pride in our tribe and our talents. This makes us dance to our best ability. Powwows have been with us a long time. This is a time to celebrate our survival.

Phillip Paul
Traditional Dancer
Flathead

There are a variety of events that take place at powwows besides dance sessions that occur in the afternoons and evenings. These can be divided into arbor and outside-the-arbor events. Arbor events include intertribal, social, exhibition, and contest dancing, drum contests, ceremonials, specials, giveaways, princess pageants, and various forms of fundraising. Events that take place outside the arbor are rodeos, parades, athletic tournaments (soft-

ball, basketball, triathlons), concession sales, gambling games, and arts and craft fairs.

There is much to do in organizing a powwow. Many people work long hours over the year to assure its success. They are the Powwow or Celebration Committee and head people.

The Committee is made up of people who are responsible for various areas of the powwow's needs, including a coordinator, secretary and treasurer, and members who take care of security, grounds, parades, concessions, pageants, publicity, registration, and contests. The Committee is made up of residents of the sponsoring reservation and when the powwow is taking place they know no sleep.

The head people comprise both honorary and professional powwow participants. They can be members of the sponsoring tribe or they can be "special guests" who are known for their abilities on the circuit. These include master of ceremony or announcer, head singer and/or host drum group, head man dancer, head woman dancer, and arena director. Some tribes also have the positions of flag bearer, drum keeper, and whipman who perform ceremonial functions.

The trick to running a good powwow is having people enjoy it. Having them go home with lots of memories, smiling, laughing, happy, and saying, "I'm gonna be back next year because I had so much fun, because the spirit was there." That's what you look for, that powwow spirit, that feeling, that friendship, that love and respect, for everyone and everything.

Boye Ladd

While the powwow committee is generally unpaid, the head people are compensated for their expenses and usually receive gifts of cash, shawls, blankets and food. Positions such as master of ceremony, head dancers and head singer are compensated enough that these people can be considered professional head people. The importance and role of the head people has increased in the past twenty years, because they attract large numbers of participants on the strengths of their reputations. They are selected early in the planning stages and their names and pictures appear on the powwow poster to ensure that people will be drawn to that event. In Oklahoma you can find both a head straight dancer and a head fancy dancer as well as head little boy or little girl dancers. The head dancers are responsible to lead off the dancers and to get people dancing. Head singers are responsible for the drum and will be discussed further in the chapter "Dancers and Drums."

The arena director helps the announcer or master of ceremony direct the events that take place within the arbor. Together they work on the schedule set up by the committee. The two of them usually handle the giveaways and specials. The arena director regulates the dancers, singers, and activities on the dance floor, making sure that eagle feathers are treated with respect when they are dropped. Arena directors also choose judges, give

FACING PAGE: Bumper stickers prevail on powwow vans.
BELOW: Maggie White participates thoughtfully in the
Windy Boy Family giveaway.

Spiritualism is very much alive and we see a lot of it on the powwow circuit. As long as there are trees and streams and nature, the beauty of the land, birds and animals, herbs and medicines, the Indian will never die. We learn to respect such things, they are part of life and religion. With them we still have ways to teach our children.

Boye Ladd, Fancy Dancer
Winnebago

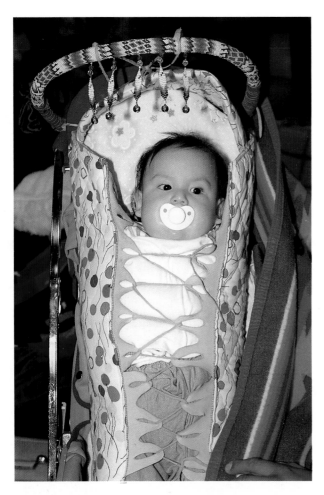

out ballots and correctly take numbers during contests. Due to the formality that exists in southern powwows, whereby the dancers and singers usually don't leave the dance floor once the session has started, the arena director will also see to it that they receive refreshments.

The powwow is a form of inner prayer for everybody 'cause everybody needs a prayer. For yourself, for people that aren't there with you, the ones that are sick at home, that can't make it to the powwow. A good song makes you feel good, makes you dance hard, then you pray for everybody.

The powwow is a big heart, as big as that dancing circle out there. That heart is beating stronger and stronger. Encampments are gettin' bigger and bigger, more people pumping life into that heart. If you treat the powwow good it will treat you good. It will get you where you want to go; you abuse it, it will abuse you. It is a powerful thing, the

powwow. It's a circle, the center of the universe. Respect it. Powwow people are one family and they will take care of you wherever you go. You will have a place to eat and a place to stay.

Joe Sam Scabby Robe Jr.
Grass Dancer
Blackfeet

My interpretation of the powwow is that it is a sharing, loving, helping one another. You become family, that's how I look at powwow. It's friendship, respecting one another, pride and patriotism.

The powwow is not a religion and it bothers me to see newcomers try to make it so. It is its own circle. A powwow circle is different from a medicine circle. The powwow is a social event.

A gathering of people to have a good time celebrating Indian customs and traditions, Indian ways. We pray in both circles, prayer is part of our life, but our medicine is made in its circle. Our socializing is done at powwows. Touch the powwow and the powwow touches every walk of life, every profession, everything that you do. You'll see the powwow relevant to it in some way.

Boye Ladd

Beadwork and blankets cover a horse trailer to make a parade float at Crow Fair.

Powwow Events

Ka-blam! The shot punctuated the mid-morning quiet. The cannon's sharp report indicated the powwow parade had started down the dusty wind-blown streets of Browning, Montana.

A beautiful morning, without a cloud in the brilliant blue sky, enabled the snow-capped Rocky Mountains to glow wintry white, providing an intense backdrop for the parade wending its way west down mainstreet. Midsummer weather bestowed the Blackfeet with a beautiful day while they celebrated North American Indian Days.

Parades

Parades are part of powwows and one of the major events of the weekend. Most of them take place on Saturday morning; the Crow parade around their encampment on all four days of Crow Fair. Powwow parades attract floats, horseback riders, marching units, bands, clowns and dignitaries. The floats usually consist of a pickup truck, car or van draped in blankets and quilts, with beadwork and costume pieces completely covering the vehicle. Princesses perch on hoods and roofs waving and throwing candy. Flatbed trucks carry entire singing groups and dancers of all ages. Horses wear beaded trappings, their war-bonneted riders display national, state and tribal flags. Women riders wear beaded buckskin dresses or fancy western attire. Color and tradition flourishes everywhere. The old and the new both present themselves.

Rodeo

Another big attraction at powwows is Indian

The greatest thing I have ever gotten out of the powwow is friends. People that really care for one another. I see it when they are worried that I eat or drink. When I go to a new place, people ask me if I need anything. They know what I need. They give me money for gas. They feed me. They tell me I look good dancing. They wish that I place in the dance contest. These things they say and do make me feel good. Make me drive many miles in the hot sun to return to them. Make me get up and dance and enjoy myself.

James Watt, Traditional Dancer
Blackfeet

BELOW: Beaded belt buckles to suit any taste.
FACING PAGE: Elders in a classic automobile at Crow Fair.

rodeo. Strong similarities exist between the pow-wow's dance events and the rodeo. Participants in both events parade into the arena in a "Grand Entry." Competitors display numbers and are judged for abilities. The events are coordinated and announced at a speaker's stand. Usually participants don't cross over between the two events, but there are a few exceptions like Phillip Whiteman, Jr., a Northern Cheyenne, who wins at saddle bronc riding and grass dancing.

Gambling

Gambling maintains its popularity at northern powwows. Wall tents pitched alongside the concessions draw poker and blackjack players. By far, stick game or hand game ranks as the most traditional and premier form of gambling. At most celebrations a stick game area is set aside for the teams' use. This usually takes the form of a roof covered mini-arbor.

Stick game consists of two teams of male and female players usually numbering between 10 to 15 members. Each team takes turns hiding two sets of marked and unmarked "bones." Correct guesses of the unmarked bone are tallied by specially marked "sticks." When a team guesses correctly they win a chance to hide the bones. If the bones are already in their possession and the other team guesses incorrectly, they win a stick. When one team wins all eleven sticks the game ends and bets are paid. Players sit in opposing rows singing stick game songs, keeping beat on hand drums or long wooden poles, while one member hides the bones. According to Woody Kipp, a Blackfeet, "the songs are songs of power which are meant to confuse the opposing side, preventing them from guessing correctly."

The guessing team uses an intricate variety of hand signals to indicate which hand holds the unmarked bone. Certain people are designated as pointers to catch the hiders. The hiders rock in rhythm to the songs, juggling the bones under shawls, hats, scarves, and behind their backs to throw the pointers off. Games usually last an hour, but can run three hours or more. Many teams play at the same time and the clacking sounds of stick game continues day and night.

Concessions

Concession stands abound at northern powwows. They sell food, arts and crafts, books and tapes, raw materials for costume making, and a variety of toys and trinkets. At larger events the concession stand area resembles a carnival midway. There are two main locations for these stands. The more traditional location rings the stands about fifty feet from the outside of the arbor, creating a walkway where people "cruise" on foot. The second sets them away from the arbor in a circle of their own. No vehicles or horses clutter this area. The powwow committee rents space to the concession-

45

The powwow is never going to die out. The only way that could happen is if Indian people die. They've both grown in number, though it is a shame that it takes so much money to host a powwow. Most of it is tied up in prizes. It should be like the old days when the money went into the camps. Spent on tipis, rations and feasts. I'd like to see the dance prizes be more than money. Something you can keep.

James Watt, Traditional Dancer
Blackfeet

Randall Blaze's pottery shows a sense of humor at the Art and Crafts Fair—United Peoples Pow Wow, Missoula, Montana.
INSET: *No powwow is complete without plenty of fry bread.*

aires, which helps defray the cost of the powwow.

During the dance sessions the concession area jams with people of all ages who buy food and drink, check out beadwork, look for the newest audio tape release of a "hot" drum group. Children chase each other, while teens and young adults "walk 'round" visiting with friends. Traffic flows both ways around the circle making it easier for people to spot one another.

Food choices range from hamburgers and fries, hot dogs, soups and stews, to the ever-present and popular fry bread. Participants encamped on the grounds enjoy "going over to the stands" in the morning hours when spectators are still home. This quiet time enables then to browse craft stands, or chat with friends over a cup of coffee or a ham and eggs breakfast with tortillas and toast. Many food stands erect awnings over picnic tables, attracting additional customers and encouraging repeat business.

Some major powwows, like the Red Earth Pow Wow in Oklahoma City, are incorporating large arts and craft fairs. No powwow is complete without craft booths. Here you find raw materials for costume construction: feathers, furs, tanned skins, porcupine quills, beads and bells. Crafts people sell beaded items like belts, buckles, handbags, barrettes and moccasins. Full costume pieces command high prices and the powwow provides an important source for a dancer's costume needs. Bustles, headdresses, even complete beadwork sets are sold or traded.

Native crafts people spearhead the forefront in perpetuating their culture and are as responsible as dancers and singers in the expansion of artistic values. Feelings among some of these crafts people indicate that the sale of trinkets and non-cultural goods such as cheap toys, rock 'n' roll memorabilia, and fake Indian-styled items should be limited to reduce the carnival-like atmosphere that exists alongside the cultural event.

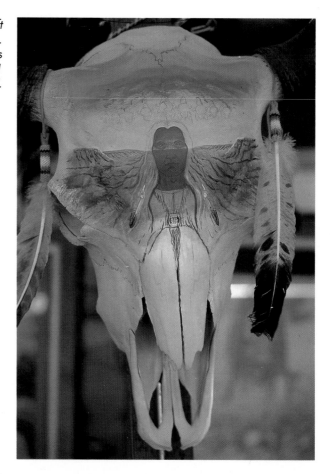

Dwayne Desjarlais commented in Canada's native *Windspeaker* magazine, "Many tribal pow-wows create a discontent with the atmosphere that prevails along the fringes of traditionalism taking place on the dancing grounds. A solution to this could be to set up regulations similar to these of international trade shows where crafts people are required to sign a contract specifying that their items are hand-crafted and genuine and only those such items sold.

"Indian people are concerned with their culture and are adopting contemporary ways to insure its strength and continuance." Dwayne went on, "Singers, dancers, and crafts people are a team working together to retain our cultural ways. This team approach is the key towards the proper and successful representation of our heritage at cultural events in the future."

Athletic Events

Tribes and powwow committees follow contemporary trends towards physical fitness. Athletic events are encouraged. Fun runs, triathlons, softball, and basketball tourneys find their way onto the powwow program. Tribes and tribal organizations sponsor teams to compete in softball in the summer and basketball in the winter. Turnouts for these events grows larger yearly.

Feasts and Feeds

Families host feasts in honor of a person or event and invite visitors to "come and eat." "Feeds" generally take place on Saturday afternoon between the afternoon and evening dance sessions. The host family will announce that the feed "welcomes visitors" over at so and so's camp and "everyone is invited to come over and get a plate." Guests line up at tables and tailgates, filling their plates with soup, stew, boiled meat, vegetables, fruits, fry bread, and dessert. Some stay and visit and others take their plates back to their own camp. Many times the host family will not know all the people they feed. Smaller informal hospitality feeds happen throughout the camp with one host family inviting other families to their camp.

Arbor Events

The arbor on the northern circuit centers the camp and the dance circle is surrounded by bleachers and covered by an overhead shade. Traditionally this shade consists of a framework covered with tree boughs, but some contemporary arbors use plywood roofs and sides for wind protection, while others are metal pavilions. The metal-roofed pavilions have the advantage of being good rain shelters, but dancers prefer open-air arbors because they have grass surfaces, better natural light, and far greater air circulation. The announcer's stand sits to the west and entry points mark the four compass directions. Lights illuminate the dance area at night.

On the southern circuit, many powwows take place in parks and rodeo grounds. The dance circle

The contemporary powwow, while social in many aspects, retains an aura of spiritual endeavor fostered by our concept of the sacred natural world. All created beings are held to be a minuscule representation of the Creator's power. Our ancient belief is that the drumbeat represents the "heartbeat of the universe." To dance to the drumbeat puts one in balance with the unseen creative forces of life.

Woody Kipp, Grass Dancer
Blackfeet

forms by placement of benches on which the participants sit. Dancers mark their places with blankets or shawls. The spectators either sit in bleachers or lawn chairs set up outside the benches. The head drum group sets up at the center of the dance circle and visiting drums set up at the edge of the circle. Up north, drum groups ring the outer edge of the dance circle, their location indicated by numbers on arbor support posts.

Grand Entry

The main powwow dance sessions begin with a parade of dancers, called the Grand Entry. Men, women and children enter by category of dance style, usually from the east entrance. The dance committee notes the competitive dancer's numbers at this time. Points are awarded for participation in this spectacular and emotional event.

> *It's an indescribable feeling when Grand Entry begins. A feeling of excitement. When I hear the song, drumbeat, bells, and war whoops and see the bustles floating by, and the children's happy faces gleaming, my whole body tingles. The sounds of Grand Entry make me feel good. It is worth all the sweat I'll make while dancing my absolute best. Dancing in the Grand Entry is the greatest time of the powwow. That's when I am at my greatest best.*
>
> Dana Runs Above
> Jingle Dress Dancer
> Assiniboine

Leading the Grand Entry, flag bearers carry the U.S. and Canadian flags, the state flag, tribal flags, and the Indian flag. The traditional and ceremonial Indian flag symbolizes Indian people and consists of a crook staff covered with cloth and fur, and hung with eagle feathers. An honored veteran

*A color guard for the United States and Blackfeet Nation flags
at North American Indian Days.*

proudly carries the flag and places it in the center of the dance circle.

Adult male traditional dancers (straight dancers in the southern circuit), parade behind the flags, followed by fancy dancers, grass dancers, women's traditional, women's fancy and jingle dress, all followed by the children's categories. When all the dancers arrive in the arena the dance session is opened with a prayer, singing of the flag song (Indian equivalent of the national anthem), the posting or retreating of colors, and welcoming words by various dignitaries.

Intertribals

The host drum starts off the first intertribal song of the dance session. Everyone is raring to go, warmed up and sweaty from the grand entry and ready to show their best dance style. Intertribal dances allow all tribes, styles, ages and genders to dance together while no judging takes place. Dancers circle the arena spying and shaking hands with acquaintances they haven't seen for a while, dancing in line for the pleasure of old friends, or dancing in place close to the drum, letting the music move them.

> *Women started coming out onto the dance floor and accepted into dance circles around 1953-54. They were never permitted on the dance floor before that time. They'd stand in the background, usually behind the drums, and sing.*
>
> Boye Ladd
> Fancy and Exhibition Dancer
> Winnebago

Ceremonials and Specials

These events take place between intertribals. The ceremonials consist of Honor Songs and giveaways. The giveaways can also be referred to as "spe-

Traditional dancers listen to the conclusion of the opening ceremonies at Rocky Boy's Memorial Pow-Wow.

cials." Specials are usually other forms of dancing besides the intertribals and the social dances. Exhibition dances are the primary form of special dances. The Hoop Dance is the most common exhibition, though various tribal dances can be seen at both northern and southern powwows.

Honor Songs are sung to honor a particular person or persons. It is customary to stand in silence showing respect during an Honor Song. Many times the song precedes a giveaway honoring a person that recently passed away. Veterans or people who have distinguished themselves also receive the honor of such songs.

We never forget the warriors, the veterans. Without the warriors we wouldn't have the freedom we have today...have this coming together, the drum, the feathers, the honor dances, all things that are part of the powwow.

Boye Ladd

Giveaways honor deceased family members. Many times Honor Dances precede giveaways, led by singers with hand drums. Family members display pictures of the deceased and the entire group circles the arena once. As it passes, friends of the family join the parade and by the time a circuit is completed the entire dance floor may be filled.

The family then produces goods they are giving away. The announcer calls out names of people "to receive a gift." Gifts take the form of blankets, quilts, cloth, money, food, horses, and tipis. Recipients shake hands with family members in a receiving line. Giveaways take a long time. There has been some criticism currently circulating among participants who travel a long distance to dance, that giveaways can cut too much into dance time. Critics suggest conducting giveaways in the mornings, between sessions or on earlier or later days of the powwow, since they are mostly an activity of the host tribe.

Giving is an important part of being Indian. To give somebody something is a good feeling. To receive a gift is another good feeling...Things are different now because we live separate, we don't go to other people's homes as much, we don't hunt and eat together as we used to. A long time ago if you were a friend you lived with us, you'd eat and visit with us. We gave to each other. Now we have the powwow. We come together as family and visitors. The powwow is at the center of giving. It is the heart of the Indian people.

James Watt
Traditional Dancer
Blackfeet

When the Feather Falls

The eagle, often represented by the Thunderbird, is treated with the highest respect by all tribes. The Thunderbird is said to be the messenger of the Creator. Indian people treasure eagle feathers. Dancers perform a special ceremony when an eagle feather accidentally drops on the dance floor. The feather is immediately pointed out and a veteran dances close by, protecting it from trampling. The dance ends, a traditional drum sings a "Brave Man" or veteran song. The arena cleared, four veteran traditional dancers perform the picking up ceremony. A veteran who has been wounded in combat is selected as the "Brave Man" and picks the feather up with another eagle feather. He then takes the microphone and recounts a war deed or special story about his military service. The "Brave Man" then returns the feather to its owner. The owner gives a gift to the man and the drum in honor of the service they have performed. This ceremony can cover all other eagle feathers falling to the floor during the evening, or be repeated.

Stick game and hand gestures meant to confuse the players.

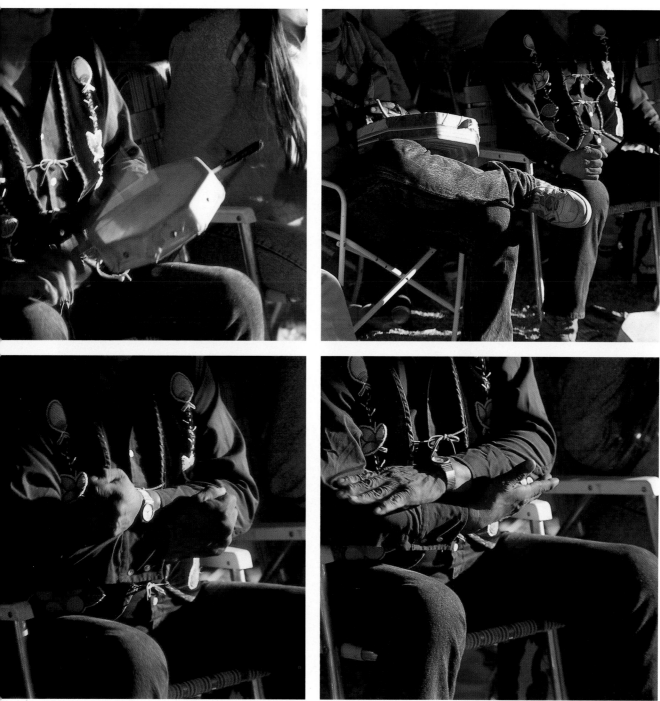

Walter Runs Above competes in fancy dance.

Nowadays there are many more white guys coming to powwows. They need to be aware of our values and culture to avoid mistakes. They need to be polite. Picture taking for example. They get in the way. Many times I have seen them complain because dancers are in front of them. They can't see what they want without moving. They tell the dancer to move. We dancers get the rough end of the stick. We are not sitting in the shade of the bleachers. No, we are wearing dance clothes out in the hot sun and dust and they are yelling at us to move.

James Watt, Traditional Dancer
Blackfeet

Photographing

During the Dropped Eagle Feather Dance, the emcee will request no photographs be taken, as during ceremonial dances, certain Honor Dances or during prayers. There is no objection to photographing parades, intertribals, and contest dances. Showing respect, visitors ask permission and offer to send copies to their subjects. They will ask permission to photograph camp scenes, and use common sense in being courteous and polite.

Some white people are all over the dancers with their cameras. I've run into them. They have run into me. They are not so polite. They want that picture, just something to take home. They're not interested in your name, your tribe, if you are hot, or sweaty, or thirsty. These people need to be educated in the values of caring for one another. If they are gonna visit another culture they need to stop and realize they are on our grounds. They should move slowly, get to know us. They shouldn't just point their camera and shoot. They are just "taking a picture" and it's not going to mean anything besides what they spent on film, just to say "I was there." Walk over to that dancer and learn something from him, he may become your friend. Then both cultures benefit, both become respectful. When you study our culture and learn from us then it's not like you first took our land, and then our pictures.

James Watt

Exhibitions

The most popular form of exhibition dancing is hoop dancing. This dance has been attributed to the southwest pueblo tribes but evidence exists that northern plains medicine men danced with circular hoops for medicinal purposes and visionary powers.

These "magical rings," while creating formations, were symbolic of the "natural forces" being called upon. Today hoop dancers create intricate shapes with 10 to 20 unconnected hoops or perform a variety of complicated dance steps and body movements with smaller hoops. Each dancer has an original routine and the dance requires much practice.

The Eagle Dance also spread northward from the southwest pueblos. The dancer wears a costume that resembles an eagle complete with head, tail, and wings. These cover the dancer's own head and arms. Executed well, this graceful dance tells the legend of an eagle's life, death, and rebirth.

Exhibitions include the performance of tribal dances from various cultural regions. These include Apache Mountain Spirit Dances, northwest coast Bear and Raven dances, various southwest pueblo dances, including a dancer demonstrating bird calls and telling stories. In the summer of 1990 Aztecs from Mexico City thrilled northern plains audiences with their fast-paced dancing, flashy costumes, flaming headdresses, and enormous exotic feathers.

Contest dance styles will be singled out for exhibitions. The announcer may ask "all male traditional dancers," or "all jingle dress dancers" to "get out there and show your stuff." Later other styles will be selected. At these times the spectators can appreciate the differences in style and observe a spectacle of color and movement while watching their favorite performers. Competitive dancers can dance their best and catch the eye of judges that may be in the audience.

Social Dances

Social dances encourage everyone present to participate. They include the Round Dance and the Owl Dance. Costumes are not required to dance in these social dances. Audience members, Indian and non-Indian alike, will come out on the dance floor and join the Round Dance circle.

Dancers move in rows of circles clockwise around the dance circle. The Owl Dance is similar to the Round Dance, except in this dance couples partner up to "lady's choice." Another couples dance is the Sioux Rabbit Dance. These will be discussed further in the chapter "Dancers and Drums."

Anybody can get out on the dance floor as long as they respect it. Some dancers are over thirty and just starting, many are just kids. Age doesn't matter. Kids around powwows all their lives feel the powwow within them. Other people only hear the music a couple of times, and the feeling is there already. They want to participate. The powwow is that much and that little. A feeling of participation, nothing else and everything else.

Tony Brown
Hoop and Fancy Dancer
Sioux-Oneida-Flathead

Indian children are vital to powwows. Their presence is an integral part of all aspects of the celebration. These young participants ensure the continuation of songs, dances, cultural heritage, and traditional ways of Indian people. Parents are more relaxed with their children. Children, in turn, are free to run and roam more than in white society.

I can go anywhere with my kids in the United States and Canada and never feel safe until I come to the powwow. There I will feel safe and not worry about somebody stealing them, or shooting them, or whatever. I really feel safe with my family when it comes to the powwow. Indian people look after their children and each other.

Tony Brown

Some children were born "powwow babies." Other children are introduced to it in their later years. Our children are "powwow babies"—that's all they've ever known. It's a part of their life. I've always encouraged them to be good participants, make friends, respect dancers and singers. I encourage them to shake elders' hands and let them know it's good they are still part of the powwow. Our children have established real close bonds with other children and their parents from all over the U.S. and Canada. We've encouraged them to be good sports about contests. If they don't place well maybe next weekend.

Dana Runs Above

Contest Dances

The most colorful event at powwows is the competition dancing that attracts spectators and participants alike to the afternoon and evening sessions of the final two days. The more serious dancers save their best moves and strongest efforts for these contest dances. Dancers are judged according to age groups, costume and/or dance style. Dancing off beat, dropping a part of an outfit, or failing to stop on the last beat of the drum can disqualify a contestant.

Contest dancing is like a job. Times are hard. There is little employment on the reservation. The money involved helps us make a living. Dancing becomes a profession. If a family works at it, all are involved and have talent, they can average four thousand dollars a month. Where on the reservation can you make that kind of money? My family is on the circuit seven months a year.

Kip White Cloud
Traditional Dancer
Sioux

Years ago tribes came together to be with friends and family again. That continues today in the powwow. We come together to celebrate, to dance, barter and trade. Today it's all modern, but it still keeps the old term. You got your concession stands here, people who buy and sell whatever. We are still split up as tribes and we still come together once or twice a year.

James Watt, Traditional Dancer
Blackfeet

"One of the hardest jobs at the powwow is judging the dance contests," declared Canadian Blackfeet elder Alex Scalplock. The 63-year-old said few judges understand how difficult it is to determine how to give or take points away from a dancer. "The common mistake is missing the beat of the drum. Many judges don't seem to think it is important, but it's the most important thing," said Scalplock, who frequently judges at powwows.

The drummers try to confuse the dancer, but the really good dancers are not tricked because they listen to the beat. For instance, trick songs are introduced to catch the dancers off guard. In order to anticipate a sudden stop, a dancer must really know the contest songs well.

I don't worry about prize money. I know I can win. Right now I am broke. I could win here [Browning, MT], big money, and be broke again next week. I'm not in it for the money, makes me feel good to go around and make people feel good watching me dance. Say to me, "Jeez, you looked good out there, had good moves, stopped right on the drum." Makes me feel good it made them feel good.
Joe Sam Scabby Robe, Jr.
Grass Dancer
Blackfeet

There are several dance categories for both men and women, teens and children. These are determined by their costume style. They are Fancy Dance, Traditional, Straight Dance in the southern powwows, Grass Dance, and Jingle Dress.

[In 1990] the Blackfeet gave out trophies as well as money for the dance contests. That was good. Something to remember. Money is just money, you spend, it's gone and forgotten.

Say you win something like a jacket, a quilt, a blanket, or a trophy. It's gonna remind you that you won something. That's respect for the dancers. Everyone cares more.
James Watt

Drum Contests

Drum group contests enhance a powwow because they attract top-quality singing groups. This in turn draws good dancers who come to dance to the best "rawhide orchestras."

The competing drum groups register and are assigned numbers or positions around the inner circle of the arbor. They must number at least five singers and cannot recruit "drum hoppers" (free-lance singers who go from drum to drum). The groups take turns singing in rotation clockwise around the arbor for intertribals, and social dances, and counter-clockwise for contests.

Each group chooses the best songs, either their own compositions, or popular songs of the circuit. Judging is by audience members and preselected judges assigning points throughout the length of the powwow.

Hand Drum contests consist of two to five singers who keep time on hand drums, as opposed to the big dance drums. They are judged by a panel of judges for their singing ability and choice and quality of song.

Princess Contests

Princess contests allow young ladies to represent their various communities or cultural clubs. Though no such concept as royalty exists in the Indian world, Princesses, First Runner-

The powwow is a spiritual experience without being a religious one. The powwow helps us to see ourselves. There's self-respect at a powwow, tribal respect, national respect, respect for the powwow life, respect for being Indian. Religion blends into the powwow. Elders pray to open dance sessions. When asked to pray, we have the same feeling in our hearts. We give thanks in our individual way. We say the same prayer only with different words, different languages. One race, one people celebrating ourselves.

Tony Brown, Fancy Dancer
Oneida-Sioux-Flathead

ups, and Attendants are called such. This term originated from early white settlers in the eastern. U.S. and Canada. In order to gain favor they referred to daughters of Indian leaders as "princesses." It is not uncommon to encounter a blond, blue-eyed non-Indian who claims descendancy from a "Cherokee princess." Once in use, the term went with the tribes to Oklahoma and spread north from there.

Powwow "royalty" wear beaded crowns and their titles are embroidered on sashes and shawls. This contest is a form of achievement, goal orientation, and good-natured rivalry. The girls are judged on poise, communication skills, knowledge of their culture and customs, a talent, and in more than a few cases, the number of raffle tickets they sell raising money for the powwow.

The contests don't always take place in the arbor but the princesses and their attendants are presented during opening ceremonies. If judging takes place during the powwow the finalists may demonstrate their talent to all the people present in the arbor.

I am very proud of my daughter Winona Rose Runs Above. Her being selected as the 1990-91 Red Bottom Pow Wow Junior Princess honors our family. A descendant of Walter Clark I, the man who started the powwow, and a descendant of Northern Cheyenne Chief Little Wolf, she also honors her ancestors. She lives up to her Indian name of "Little Wolf Woman."

Dana Runs Above

Fundraising Activities

Prior to, and during the powwow, fundraising activities occur regularly. Money is needed for prizes, rations, grounds improvement, security, sanitation, and to assist singers with travel ex-

BELOW: A Fort Belknap princess dances in a jingle dress competition.
FACING PAGE: At a giveaway on the Blackfeet reservation.

The powwow means, that I, Joe Sam Scabby Robe, Jr., brother of Kenny Scabby Robe, son of Joe Sam Scabby Robe, Sr., carry on my father's background. In so doing I keep his name alive. His body is gone but his soul, his spirit, is still here with us. My brother and I represent our father. If one person in a family carries on the traditions, then the whole family carries on. The powwow is a continuation of family, and the family generates powwow life.

James Watt, Traditional Dancer
Blackfeet

penses. Bingo raises big money in both the north and south. Games held all winter and spring are well attended.

During the powwow additional money needs to be raised to help stranded travelers, compensate exhibition dancers, honor a drum group for a special song, and continue to defray costs.

A variety of activities helps meet these needs. Blanket dances are common, and everyone contributes by throwing money into a blanket carried by "royalty" around the arbor. Children particularly like running up and throwing loose change or dollar bills into the blanket. Fifty-fifties consistently raise money, with playing cards torn in half sold as chances in a drawing. The winner receives half the pot from the sale of a deck of cards.

Raffles are another money maker, with prizes obtained and tickets sold throughout the powwow grounds. Close to the end of the last day the winning numbers are announced and the holders of those tickets can claim beadwork, buckskin, blankets, guns, meat (half a beef or a haunch of buffalo), shawls, tipis, horses and cars. Auctions sell off artwork, costume pieces, or the same items as raffles.

Powwows run in a different time zone. This has nothing to do with geography. "Indian time" is prevalent at most Indian social activities. A non-Indian definition of "Indian Time" describes this phenomenon as "a total disregard for clocks, watches and time in general, a complete indifference to promptness." Indian people say, "Things start when they start and end when they end." Gloria Young wrote in her Ph.D. dissertation, "Time need not be filled with activity, it may just 'be.' Indian people know how to sit still and enjoy things, how to look even when there is nothing to see. Indians feel no compulsion to fill time with words." "Indian time" relaxes; watches are

ignored. Without the fear of being late, a sense of timelessness treats everyone to a pressureless environment. Be prepared to enjoy that feeling.

Indians believe that Hell is today. So we try to take every day with ease. We believe that when we die, it will be a happy time. To see our passed-on relations is a joyful thing.
Kip White Cloud

A powwow is a busy event filling four days. It gathers together diverse people into a community with its own services and economic base. No individual can experience all that goes on at the major celebrations throughout the U.S. and Canada. No matter how many powwows people attend, they will always experience new sights, sounds and encounters.

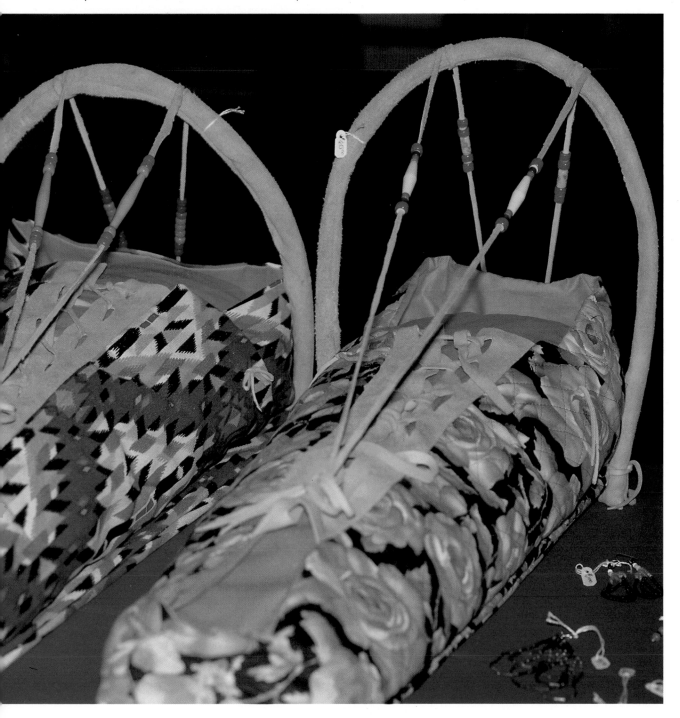

Many kinds of handmade items are on sale at powwows.

The excitement and movement of fancy dance.

Dancers and Drums

"All you dancers, let's start getting ready! Grand Entry at seven o'clock. It's contest time!" The amplified voice of Earl Old Person reverberates throughout the camp. "Drum roll call in fifteen minutes. Let's get set up; singers make your way to the arbor."

Dinner break over, a general hustle activates the camp. Mothers round up children, singers warm their voices, fancy dancers tape sore knees, and traditional dancers meticulously apply face paint. Everyone prepares for the final night of contest dancing. Dancers don their outfits carefully, making sure all ties are tight. If an object falls off, they will be disqualified. Singers tighten their drums, seeking the right sound. Spectators load their arms with blankets, chairs, tape recorders and cameras. Tonight's the big night, the finals for the adult dance contests. Thousands of dollars will reward the winning dancers and singers.

It's good to be a dancer who's looked up to. Just like growing old, the older you get, the more wisdom you have. I'm young, but I've been dancing for twenty-five years. Those years put me at a higher level of respect. I feel that from people. I never ask for it. They look at me and I can tell. They've watched me dance and understand what I feel. They know my heart is good.

Tony Brown
Fancy and Hoop Dancer
Oneida-Sioux-Flathead

66

When we dance and sing we are praising our ancestors and remembering the Creator. Even the Bible says that "when David danced before the Lord, he danced with all his might for the Lord, to give praise to him." That's what we're doing, praising our forefathers and ancestors by dancing with feelings. We let our heart extend to that bigger heart. That bigger circle. The powwow becomes the center of my universe. The drumbeat, the heartbeat of that universe.

James Watt, Traditional Dancer
Blackfeet

As powwows' popularity has increased since the civil rights movements of the 1960s and '70s, types of dances, outfits and singing styles have multiplied. And, since the early days of cash awards for dance contests, performance styles and outfits have continued to evolve. Referring to dance clothes, beadworker Sandra Ariwite of Fort Hall, Idaho, stated, "Never call our powwow clothing 'costumes.' Clowns wear costumes."

Dance outfits clearly display tribal distinctions. Sioux traditional dancers are easily separated from Cree, Sarcee, and Yakima. Flatheads prefer plateau panel leggings. Their tribal spiritual leader, Johnny Arlee, dons a traditional elk mane headdress. Umatilla women of Oregon are noted for their beaded or basket woven hats in place of crowns. Woodland tribes favor floral beadwork and excel at intricate ribbonwork. The trained eye recognizes Nez Perce, Shoshone, Arapahoe, Cheyenne, Comanche, and Mandan entering the dance floor. Southern Cheyenne women bead fine strips on white buckskin dresses, Northern Cheyennes prize full-beaded yokes. Moccasins vary in construction and design. As powwows grow in popularity and more people continue to be involved, these differences will become more pronounced. Tribal pride, awareness, and knowledge of heritage will influence and exert themselves upon individuals, continuing to create distinctive identities.

Early Fancy Dance or Feathers Outfits

As the powwow grew in the early '20s, eye-catching dance items were copied and picked up by members of various tribes. Oklahoma dancers started losing their distinct tribal characteristics and became more oriented to the particular style of fancy or feathers dance. By 1922 members of the Ponca, Pawnee, Otoe and Kiowa tribes were wearing U-shaped feather-back bustles, matching round arm bustles, and feathered head crests. They wore tights, capes, aprons, and side, knee, and ankle bells. This early fancy dance outfit did not reflect any particular tribe but was generically adopted by the dancers of the period.

The origins of bustles date back to pre-reservation times when the Omaha and Ponca wore "crow belts" in the Omaha (Hethuska) war dance. These were ceremonial belts worn at the small of the dancer's back and were constructed of hawk and eagle feathers which draped to the ankle. The headdress (deer and porcupine hair roach), said to represent the top knot of male prairie birds, also had its origins in the Omaha Dance. Other items of dance clothing—beadwork, breastplates, necklaces, leggings, anklets, moccasins—all can be traced to pre-reservation plains culture.

Indian people are adaptable, always have been. We teach our children to be that way. I don't claim to be a traditionalist. I've always heard "Take the best from both worlds, Indian and white." When I'm in a hurry I take the things that are fast from the white world, like McDonald's, or plastic instead of wood in building my dance bustles. Bright day-glow colors, too. We Indians have always borrowed from other cultures. Indians in the 1800s took the best from that time period or they wouldn't have used beads. My grandmother told me her father used to shine washers and wear them as earrings. What I make is Indian because I made it.

James Watt
Traditional Dancer
Blackfeet

The early feathers dancers had a style that was reminiscent of old plains "war dancing." This consisted of exaggerated upper-body movement and active head movements. The chest was thrown out

A Cheyenne's beaded fancy dance harness.

I'll see dancers dance towards the middle of the arena. That's to touch Mother Earth to let her know that we care and give thanks. To touch the middle of the universe and to give thanks. Powwows allow me to do this.

James Watt, Traditional Dancer
Blackfeet

Detail of John Grounds' traditional-dance outfit.

and the shoulders twisted and rocked. The head was held high and looked and moved from side to side as if searching for an enemy. The dancer had a proud, almost haughty, demeanor. This can be seen in today's traditional dancer.

During the late '40s and '50s the emphasis switched to intricate footwork. An outstanding champion in those days was Clyde Warrior. In the '60s dancers began to spin and use their bodies more. The songs continued to increase in tempo, which led the dancers to abandon the fine footwork and concentrate on spins and overall body effects. Today the Oklahoma fancy dancer concentrates on fancy footwork, energetic body work, and strong head movement to a "fast and fancy" contest song. Outfits vary from those of the northern fancy dancer in that the southern style emphasizes a cleaner, more manicured look.

Outfit Basics

All male and female dancers have certain characteristic outfit elements that vary individually with personal tastes. For males, basic elements are bustles for fancy and traditional dance (grass dancers don't wear bustles); headdresses and spreaders; beadwork (belt, harness, sidedrops, armbands, kneebands, headbands, capes and cuffs); breastplates, aprons, chokers, anklets, bells, and moccasins.

Females wear cloth or buckskin dresses, beadwork (belts, capes, crowns, hair decorations, braid wraps, leggings, moccasins), breastplates, chokers, handbags, and fringed shawls. Female dancers do not wear bells.

Both sexes and all ages always dance with hand objects. Men dance with fans, dance sticks, hoops, whistles, scarves, mirror boards, and rawhide shields, and beaded bags. Women with fans, scarves, dance sticks, and shawls.

Powwows are growing. Their growth is keeping our people together. The only way we are going to survive as a people is to join together. We've gotta survive. I can't say, "Well, I'm Sioux and you're Blackfeet, we can't get along." We can't do that. We have to put our tribal differences aside and let non-Indians know that we are one. The powwow joins us.

Tony Brown, Fancy Dancer
Oneida-Sioux-Flathead

Fancy Dance

Fancy dancers, male or female, are bright, colorful and flashy. Men wear hackle or gaily decorated eagle feather bustles on their backs while the women wear fancy embroidered shawls with long fringe to accentuate their movements. Both use intricate, fast and acrobatic motions. When a "fast and fancy" contest song is sung, the dancers strain and whirl, twisting and turning in a dazzling explosion of color.

Fancy dancer Irene Goodwill, from Saskatchewan, has an unusual method she uses to develop her winning steps. "I watch men dance in fancy dance competitions. If I see a good step or move, I put it in my routine," she explained. "You have to be in top physical shape to compete in powwows," stressed Goodwill, adding that she jogs 30 miles over five days and does aerobics. "One year I slacked off a little and I found it hard to stay in contests. It seems like over the years the emphasis by the judges is to see how many songs you can dance during a contest."

Alvin Windy Boy, champion Cree fancy dancer from Rocky Boy, Montana is a professional circuit dancer and tribal game warden. Windy Boy, 40, is a pleasant person who teaches his children cultural aspects of the powwow. If he feels he isn't in shape for the summer contests, he puts himself through rigorous training sessions as any good athlete would. "Fancy dance is just like any other sport," he explained. If you're not in good shape you are not a competitor." Windy Boy practices fancy dance for an hour each day. He works on his "moves," developing new ones that other dancers have copied.

Many fancy dancers today don't know what good footwork is. They don't know what dancing is, or balance is. Balance is left and right, figure fours, they don't know what I'm talking about.

Boye Ladd works hard in fancy dance.

If it's not written down, who's gonna believe that our culture isn't dead? Our ways were never written down. They were passed on by our elders. Non-Indians feel if it ain't proven on paper it isn't so, and if it is on paper it is. Paper burns, gets old, crumples into dust. It's much harder for a people's ways to die unless they are killed. I am glad that the powwow will be on paper, then non-Indians will know we are alive.

Tony Brown, Fancy Dancer
Oneida-Sioux-Flathead

Oklahoma style beadwork shows in Joe Bointy's fancy dance harness.

In teaching dancing I always teach lefts and rights, what you do on the left you do on the right. Balance your footwork. Try to do it in series of fours. True champions will do that. Spin four to the left, balance with four to the right. Four is our sacred number.

Boye Ladd
Fancy and Exhibition Dancer
Winnebago

When dancing intertribals, fancy dancers do not exhibit their contest style unless a particular drum group sings "a good one" and the dancer "really gets going." The dancer will dance in place, close to the drum, and "put on a show." Even then acrobatic moves are reserved for contests and the dancer primarily focuses on footwork and spins.

Fancy dancers in contests are judged on how well they have put together an exuberant style consisting of fancy footwork, high-stepping spins, and acrobatic body moves during stops, starts, and accent beats (see Drum Groups and Styles, page 85).

Johnny Whitecloud is the fancy dancer who started all those handsprings, splits, flips, pushups, you name it, he was acrobatic. Gordon Lasley had speed, smoothness, footwork. Unbelievable. Like Joe Boynte today, he floated. Joe Sam Scabby Robe floats that way above the ground as a grass dancer. He floats and moves. Good dancers hit a point where they can do no wrong, they're smooth, they have spirit, they are perfect.

Boye Ladd

Traditional dancers wear natural outfits, and are currently the major attraction of the dance contests. Men wear hawk and eagle feather bustles and bone breastplates. Their clothing utilizes more historical articles. Smoked hide leg-

Grass dancers have their numbers taken after competing.

Fancy Dance originated from early grass dance. Grass Dance is an alternate form of the way we traditionally danced. Both forms can tell a story.

Kip White Cloud, Traditional Dancer
Sioux

gings and capes, buckskin fringe, old beadwork patterns, natural as opposed to glowing colors, feather decorated dance sticks, animal (coyote or wolf) or feather headdresses typify the male traditional dancer.

> *Judges look at the outfit and how one carries his or herself with pride and dignity. The best dance outfits come from dreams and visions. We are told in this way how to put them together.*
>
> Phillip Paul
> Traditional Dancer
> Flathead

Females wear ankle length white or smoked buckskin dresses with long fringes extending from the arms of their full beaded shoulder capes. High-top beaded moccasins or leggings, beaded bags, brass tack or concho ornamented belts and sidedrops, otter braid wraps, eagle feather and plume hair ornaments, and knee-length breastplates round out the traditional women's attire.

Darlene Windy Boy, Alvin's wife, is a traditional dancer. She went to her first powwow in Detroit, Michigan. She met Alvin at a powwow in Fraser, Montana, where she was impressed with his abilities as a fancy dancer. "He could throw his dance sticks in the air, spin around, and catch them in mid-air and then stop on the last beat of the drum doing splits."

Darlene beads her family's outfits, it being too costly to purchase them; good dance outfits range upwards from $2,000. Recently turning 33, she said "When you turn older, you envision yourself dancing traditional. Even today I still get butterflies when I compete. You just have to go out there and do the best you can." Windy Boy added with enthusiasm, "I love the powwow and I'll keep going to them and see my grandchildren dance. I don't think I can spend summers any other way. It's a way of life now."

Ron Walsey, from Warm Springs, Oregon, dances traditional and travels with his children to powwows. He is excited by the changes and growth encountered in Indian cultural values over the past twenty years. "I take my children to powwows even though they are little. That is where they learn about their culture and roots." His four-year-old son stands close to him, fingering his beadwork, watching the dancers his age in the "tiny tots" division. "My daughter stayed home with her mother this weekend as we traveled a long way [to Montana] and she is only 14 months old, but she already walks and dances. The powwow is very special, something we are proud of." His son breaks away to join the others, bells ringing and braids flying.

"Traditional" male dancers throw out their chests and bend low, carefully moving their heads and bodies. They re-enact warriors searching for an enemy or hunters stalking prey. Always conscious of the story they are telling, they search the ground for tracks, constantly alert. Envision a proud rooster strutting in a barnyard, lifting his feet with grace and poise, head darting back and forth, and you see a male traditional dancer in top form.

> *Dance is telling a story, your exploits, what you saw in battle, different things you did. You step, you balance, you crouch. Dance is foot work. Dance is motion. It's what you do in dance.*
>
> Boye Ladd

> *I have been a traditional dancer since 1977. I grass danced for two years and fancy danced for seven years prior to coming out as a traditional. Fancy dancing is like a young colt, frisky, still learning the ways as it steps into life, expressing a younger spirit. It is very*

spur of the moment. Traditional is coming into manhood, very deliberate, confident and self assured.

Kip White Cloud
Traditional Dancer
Sioux

Female traditional dancers carry themselves with dignity and grace. Their subtle and precise dance steps cause the long buckskin fringe to sway in gentle harmony to their bodies. Older women will sometimes dance in one spot keeping rhythm with the drum by bobbing gently up and down while they turn their feet gently to and fro, first one way for six or seven beats and then back the other way for the same. Holding eagle feather fans, they faintly fan themselves, occasionally raising them to the sky in honor of the drum and its song.

When I see today's leading dancers, people like traditional Tim Eashappie from Fort Belknap, Montana, or Joe Sam Scabby Robe from Browning, I see a spirit of originality. A spirit that is created within themselves. Tim has his own style of dancing, he is in a class of his own. Others see it and appreciate the beauty. They copy him. People can tell between a copy and an originator, a real champion. It's like what Tim says, "Jeez, I come around a corner, I start dancing, and I almost bump into myself."

Boye Ladd

Straight Dance

Rarely seen up north, Straight Dance is popular on the southern circuit. Like all forms of "war dancing," its roots can be found in the old warrior societies. Straight dancing corresponds to traditional dance. Many fancy dance veterans switch

78

The beaded dress yoke of Cree traditional dancer
Tina Daniels.

We have our friendly rivalries. Here in Montana you hear joking between Blackfeet and Flathead or Sioux and Crow. There's traditional feelings between tribes. But as Indian people we gotta set some of that aside, we can't be feuding because in many ways we are still fighting for our rights against the rest of the world. I met this guy from North Dakota back in '69, our tribes used to always knock heads. Even though we compete for dance money we are like brothers. We are always glad to see each other.

Tony Brown, Fancy Dancer
Oneida-Sioux-Flathead

over to it in their later years. The dancers wear cloth or leather leggings "backwards" so that the decorative ribbonwork faces front. From the waist hangs front and rear aprons and a cloth trailer with matching ribbonwork. Bright satin ribbon shirts cover upper torsos. Beaded belts, woven sashes, and German silver armbands add adornment over the shirt. All straight dancers wear an "otter drop" that extends from the back of their necks to the floor. Dancers use folded handkerchief headbands, porcupine headdresses with one eagle feather in the spreader, or otter fur turbans.

The dancers weave and glide in a stately manner around the dance floor. A sideways back and forth nodding of the head replaces the rocking motions of fancy dance. Dancers carry "tail sticks" and mirror boards, crouching low and pointing to the drum during honor beats.

Crow Traditional Style

Similar to the southern plains straight dance in evolution is the modern traditional Crow style. Extremely distinctive, they are always recognizable, and can't be mistaken for other tribes. "Crows are Crows," said Walter Old Elk, a champion Crow dancer. "We are a people who pride ourselves in the differences our culture has from other plains tribes. The Crow people speak a different language, trace our heritage through our mothers, and band together in clans. Our dancing is unique and we are known for it."

The modern Crow style had its beginning in the 1920s and '30s and has seen only minor changes since the 1960s. Crows wear brocade capes and aprons over colored tights or bare skin. Long breastplates replace traditional loop necklaces. Matching appliqued beadwork sets designed in floral or geometric patterns consist of wide belts and pouches similar to women's, sidedrops, cuffs, armbands, and mirror bags. Contemporary bustles

resemble colorful feather dusters with trailers or have eagle and hawk feathers in natural tones. Around their ankles cluster large dance bells worn over athletic socks. Crow outfits are incomplete without a string of side bells. Their porcupine headdresses are worn flat. Rooster feathers tuck into rhinestone or bead headbands, from which hang braids and long beaded drops. Dancers intricately paint their faces and sometimes rouge their lips and blush their cheeks. "We Crows are a proud people," Walter Old Elk emphasized.

On the floor they dance in a straight traditional manner with a heavy emphasis on the heel, or second beat. Practicing a precise dance style, family members or friends will commonly dance in a line "following the leader." Carrying mirror bags (containing valuables) in their left hands and dance sticks in their right, their large bells ringing loudly, a line of Crow dancers can thoroughly throw off other dancers' rhythm. "They are like a freight train passing by. You can't hear the drum, only their beat. It takes awhile to collect yourself and find your step if they get too close," said Stanley Pretty Paint, one of the few Crow fancy dancers.

Grass Dance

With their popular northern dance style, grass dancers are very characteristic and recognizable because of a lack of bustles and the colored yarn fringe worn on matching shirt, pants and aprons. Porcupine headdresses command attention with eagle plume tipped wires in spreaders. Beadwork consists of a long, ground-length harness, matching belt, cuffs, armbands and headband. Large sheep bells clang noisily on the ankles.

Grass dancer Darryl Goodwill grew up into the sound of the drum. All his family participates in the powwow and today he passes on those traditions to his children. "I started to dance as a small boy, beginning seriously when I was eight," said

A Canadian traditional dancer.

Canadian Sioux grass dancer Darryl Goodwill.

Grass dancing takes a lot of effort and a different finesse. In my opinion, the hardest style is fancy. You have to have stamina, know the basics real well, be quick, agile and smooth. You have to be able to throw in surprise moves. Grass dancing has a lot of body movement as well as footwork, but a dancer can "ride," stop in one place and let the body do the dancing. There's more politics in traditional than footwork, it's an attitude that carries through the entire dancer. In fancy your body and feet have to constantly move in a smooth, fast way. It takes it out of you.

Boye Ladd, Fancy Dancer
Winnebago

Goodwill, originally from Maple Creek, Saskatchewan. At age 27 he has tried all dance types but confessed that grass dance is his favorite. "There are a lot of body movements and steps. It is very strenuous, difficult and challenging. You need a lot of energy and stamina. Grass dancers move their entire bodies in odd contortions; hips, arms, and shoulders are constantly rocking and shaking."

> *Jonathan Windy Boy, a Chippewa-Cree from Rocky Boy, could never do anything in fancy. He switched about the time others were switching to traditional. However, he came out grass dancing. Then he was in the money all the time. Joe Sam, too, he'd win a few local contests as a fancy dancer. Then he switched to grass, and boom, he found his field. He's a great dancer.*
>
> Boye Ladd

Jingle Dress

Jingle dress dancing recently experienced a rebirth in popularity. This style began among the Chippewa of Wisconsin and spread to the Sioux of North Dakota in the 1920s. In the late 1940s and early '50s it had spread westward into Montana. But by the 1960s, this dance style was rarely seen. Women started wearing jingle dresses again in the late 1970s and jingle dress dancing is the "hot new style" for women.

Jingle dresses utilize bright cloth with large tin cone "jingles" sewn in line or chevron patterns. Copenhagen chewing tobacco can lids rolled into cones make the best jingles. Dancers complete their outfits with metal concho belts, high-top beaded moccasins, and neck scarves. Heads are left bare, or decorated with a single eagle plume. Hands are empty, or sometimes hold scarves or fans, and kept close to the hips when dancing. "Jingle dressers" do not use shawls.

Dancers perform in an up-and-down motion due to the tightness of the form-fitting dress. Feet lift in a hopping, rocking manner that causes the jingles to produce a rhythmic clacking. Since female dancers do not wear bells, this style adds a pleasing sound to refined motion during contests.

> *Even though jingle dress is very popular now, it's like grass dance, it's always been here. It's a regional style that's trendy. Trends, styles and fads spread from tribe to tribe and ebb and flow in popularity. Anthropologists label this "pan-Indianism." It's the way we are, we always borrow from each other. Some tribes seeing jingle dress for the first time think it's new. Fads tend to bring old styles out, and they become "rediscovered."*
>
> Boye Ladd

Gourd Dance

Although observed on the northern circuit in the mid- and late 1980s, the Gourd Dance emanates from Oklahoma tribes and originated with the Kiowa Gourd Clan, a warrior society. Intertribal Gourd Dance societies host Gourd Dances prior to regular dance sessions. Most of the dancers are ex-servicemen and veterans of the last three wars. A gourd dancer's distinctive dance clothes consist of a red and blue blanket draped over the shoulders so that both ends hang in front, a woven sash at the waist, and bandoliers of mesquite beans or large cut glass beads worn over street clothes. In their right hands, dancers shake rattles made of gourds or German silver canisters, in their left they hold loose feathers or eagle fans. Beadwork is usually of the fine-cut bead variety associated with peyote ceremonies.

Singers stand and hold the drum above the ground or use hand drums. Women wear shawls and dance at the outer edge of the dance circle. Men dance in a stationary position, lifting their

The drum is a tool of our culture. The drum is the heartbeat of our people. All living things are in the drum. The drum can just sit there, it's dead. Life comes to it by hitting it. When you sing with the drum you are giving part of your life to it.

Dancing to the drum and the song gives more of yourself to the Creator. Our dancing is an old thing to the Creator. We dance because we are happy. It's an offering to the Creator. We say, "Look, I'm dancing, I'm giving you this, I'm giving of myself now." I think the Creator enjoys that and looks down and smiles.

James Watt, Traditional Dancer
Blackfeet

heels off the ground in beat to the drum. They dance slowly, circling around in lines or arcs, stopping at appropriate times in the song, keeping beat with their rattles.

Drum Groups and Songs

"It's the song that makes dancers want to get out there and move. The drum only helps them keep beat. Dancers key on the melody of the song. Rhythms, tones, pitch all help create their 'moves.' Good drums get the dancers out there, good songs get them to dance well. Without drum groups there is no music. No music, no dance, no powwow." Bill Runs Above knows what he talks about. In his teen years he dazzled people with his dancing, now he serenades them with his songs. Bill, a Sioux/Cheyenne from Fraser, Montana, sings with the popular groups Eagle Whistles and Badlands. A prominent fixture on the circuit, he is welcomed by any drum group "to sit at their drum." He sings on tapes and in the movies, having appeared in *Running Brave* with Robby Benson.

Bill is both a lead singer and composer of Indian music. "I'm whistling dance tunes all the time. When I'm making part of my son Walter's fancy outfit, I whistle. When I drive down the powwow highway, I whistle. Songs always run through my head. Singing is my life. I sing all the time." Bill's ability to sing takes him all over the country, and in the summer of 1991 to Carnegie Hall and to Europe to "sing Indian."

The way it used to be, it was common to know where a song came from or whose song it was. Recognition was given to who made the song. Nowadays it seems no one cares as much. If a new song is sung everyone rushes to record it. If my husband, Bill, makes a song I am sometimes the first to hear it. When I hear it sung good by another group, I

85

feel very proud. But when a drum group sings it wrong I want to tell them, "Sing it right or don't sing it. Have some respect!"

Dana Runs Above
Jingle Dress Dancer
Assiniboine

To the unfamiliar listener, Indian singing sounds exotic, different, and difficult to comprehend. To the trained ear, melodies flow, ascend and descend. Dancers react to these melodies, spinning, turning, dipping, and nodding to the key shifts in melody and structure. Northerners sing in high falsetto voices from deep in their throats, pushing sound from the diaphragm. Southerners sing with lower pitch but use the same basic song structure.

A drum is headed by one or more lead singers. Drum groups learn their songs through constant repetition. The lead singer ensures that everyone remembers the song by either humming or whistling the melody, and running through it softly before everyone sings. Most songs don't use words but employ vocables (vowel sounds of ya, hey, hi, lay, loi, etc.). These have no meaning but carry the tune of the song. They correspond to tones and notes. A lead singer "leads off" (begins) with the first line of the song's chorus. Another singer "seconds" him by repeating that line with slight variations in pitch and tone before the first line is completed. The rest of the group joins in singing all of the first chorus. Three accented drum beats indicate the break between chorus and verse. Dancers "honor the drum" at this time by bending low, hopping low if they are fancy dancers, or shifting their dance styles in certain ways. Repeating a chorus and verse four times (four "pushups") constitutes a full song. Emphasis on speed and volume on the last five beats of the song indicate its end, which allows dancers to stop right on beat. A "tail" is sung, a short repeat of the final chorus, and the song is over.

It's a medium-fast song with a good melody where a fancy dancer can really get down, move nice, do everything. It's good music that helps a good dancer show his stuff. If you give me a stink song, I'll dance stink. If you give me good music, I'll give you a great show.

Boye Ladd

Entire extended families, relations, and friends comprise both northern and southern drum groups. In the south the Head Drum sets up in the center of the dance floor with the men drumming and women sitting behind them, singing high harmonies to the chorus and verse. A public address microphone is suspended over the drum for amplification. Other drums set up on the outer periphery.

Drum etiquette receives great importance on the southern circuits. The drum serves as the central symbol of Oklahoma powwows. Located in the middle of the dance arena, it is suspended above the ground by four upright holders representing the four directions. Singers are restricted by protocol from casually leaving and returning to the drum. The drum is honored with gifts of tobacco during giveaways and the recipients acknowledge gifts by standing. Water boys bring drinks to singers, as propriety dictates they remain with the drum until it is carried out at the close of the session. The respect it receives illustrates the modern southern drum's relation to earlier religious dances.

In the north, drums set up on the periphery of the circle with the host drum being in the number one position. In the mid-'70s women started drumming with the men and often "second the song."

A drum group's equipment consists of the rawhide-headed drum, a cloth bag filled with padded drum sticks, drum stand, folding chairs, and a public address system. Eagle feathers, fur, flags, and

*The Kicking Woman Singers, a Blackfeet Drum group led
by Maynard Kicking Woman.*

strips of colored cloth embellish boomed micro-phones. Painted designs decorate speakers. Drum heads sometimes display elaborate painted designs, signatures of members, or list powwows attended.

Singers name themselves after families like Eagleman and Kicking Woman, geographic locations like Chiniki Lake, Chief Cliff, Stoney Park, Badlands, or Blackfoot Crossing, tribal societies like Morning Star, Young Grey Horse, or Black Lodge, or colorful names like Teton Travelers, Haystack Ramblers and Eagle Whistles. Group names adorn satin jackets, baseball caps, panel vans, and chair backs.

Songs vary in purpose and desired effect. Contest songs, like Trick Songs, stop and start suddenly. A ruffle of rapid beats indicates a Shake Song. Pronounced, slow-paced beats have dancers Crow Hop. Traditionals tell war stories and re-enact brave deeds to Sneak Up songs. Southerners enjoy Snake, Stomp, and Buffalo dances. Rabbit Dances and Two-Steps join partners north and south. Intertribal, traditional, grass, and fancy dance songs range in tempo from slow to super fast, while social dance songs like the Round Dance, Owl Dance and "49s" employ a medium one-two beat. Honor, Victory, Veteran, and Flag Songs elicit emotion, respect and reverence.

Several years ago singers like Black Lodge and Chiniki Lake started to incorporate native language words into intertribal and contest dance songs. This new style rapidly caught on in the northern plains and as this popular form spreads east and west, "word songs" crop up everywhere.

Just like in the modern non-Indian world of music there are…different styles in powwow music. Intertribals have "straight" [older] songs and "word" songs. Both are good. Straight songs remind me of old rock 'n' roll, sung by older groups. Younger groups start-ing up like to sing the word songs. This reminds me of pop music, popular with the younger generation. They still have that beat and they still make you dance, but it's nice to hear that "good old rock 'n' roll" song you remember so well. Straight singing is that way.
Dana Runs Above

If you compare dance styles and costuming, even footwork, to what existed thirty or forty years ago, there's no comparison. You can't match today's costuming to what existed in the fifties, sixties and early seventies. There's thousands of dollars and countless hours in these outfits and good dancers practice and train constantly. All the good groups have re-corded tapes available to train to. What we've got today is the best.

Boye Ladd

Crow Fair, when Crow Agency, Montana, calls itself the "Tipi Capital of the World."

Encampments

"Outdoor powwows," commented Blackfeet grass dancer Woody Kipp, "enable people to experience what is left of traditional Indian camp life. Indoor powwows are limited in scope. Their focus is on the dance. Outdoor powwows are different altogether. Tipis erected around the dance arbor become home for the duration of the powwow.

"The outdoor powwow is a happy affair, with kids running and playing, dogs barking, dancers going to and fro from camp to arbor and back again. In the encampments you will find many people who participate primarily as campers, savoring the chance to relive a portion of their old buffalo-hunting lifestyle," he added.

Young riders park their chrome-plated "war ponies"—motorcycles—outside painted tipis. Dusty, dented cars, mud-spattered pickups, and battered vans vie for space with air-conditioned motorhomes, travel trailers, and state-of-the-art tents. Horses, a more traditional mode of transportation, are everywhere. The powwow grounds pulsate with life and activity. The camp, an exciting and enjoyable place, beckons visitors to make themselves welcome.

Since reservations do not exist in Oklahoma, many of their powwows take place in temporary locations. Community parks and rodeo grounds serve as powwow grounds. Powwows sponsored by non-reservation northern plains intertribal organizations utilize the same kinds of locales that southern ones do. Where host tribes are located on reservations, established powwow grounds have their own space and facilities for encampments.

The northern plains stretch for hundreds of miles east of the Rocky Mountains. In the spring

and summer, before drought parches the land golden brown, it is lush with greenery. River bottoms and valleys supply moisture to the grasses and cottonwood trees that mark their locations. A constant breeze blows, freshening the air. The limitless sky is often an azure blue for days. Reservations are isolated on vast tracts of undeveloped land and powwow committees locate grounds in sheltered, naturally inviting areas that were traditional tribal campsites.

Crow Fair, the largest encampment in the northern plains, spreads through a two-mile-wide grove of towering cottonwood trees alongside the Little Big Horn River. This huge area utilizes paved circular roads to direct campers to the various subcamps in which reservation districts pitch hundreds of tipis. In the center of camp, the 200-foot-diameter dance arbor attracts a ring of concessions around its outside perimeter. Encircling the central camp area, a black-topped road provides the route for the Crows' daily parades. Rows of tipis erected with freshly cut poles, many with greenery on their tips, emanate from this heart. This is "Tipi Capital of the World," and for four days home to 15,000 people.

Standoff, Alberta hosts Kainai Indian Days in Red Crow Park on the banks of the Belly River. Hundreds of trees provide welcome shade to every camp. Arlee's Fourth of July Celebration on the Flathead Reservation, one of the most beautiful grounds in the western states, sits at the base of Montana's majestic Mission Mountains, nestled in the serene Jocko Valley. In the heart of the Washington's fertile Columbia Basin, surrounded by vineyards and hops, White Swan attracts visitors and participants to several powwows a year. Browning, Montana, dazzles the eyes with sweeping vistas and spectacular sunsets over the Rocky Mountains of Glacier National Park. Rocky Boy's encampment to the east hugs a ridge top in the foothills of the

Bear Paw Mountains. Each camp is unique unto itself and part of the attraction of that particular powwow.

Camp Features

It's said by Indian people that "it takes three ingredients to make a powwow. The first of course, is Indians. The second is dust, so fine that it covers everything and gets everywhere. Eyes are red with it, hair is thick with it, food is gritty with it. The third is dilapitated, overflowing outhouses." Fortunately the first ingredient is ever-increasing, as more Indian people recognize their heritage and participate in the powwow. Fortunately also, modern technology improves the second two.

The dance arbor serves as the primary camp feature, where major events are centered. They range in diameter from 100 to 200 feet, with speakers' stands are the centerpoint of the arbor and are usually located to the west. These are constructed like small sheds with a large window space facing inwards, allowing the announcers to see the arena

Stick game arbor, Arlee, Montana.

activities. Inside these stands are the dance registrars and powwow officials. A public address system enables the emcee to announce events, raffle winners, lost articles, and found children. Stands receive white paint to reflect the sun's rays and have powwow posters tacked in strategic locations announcing upcoming events. Flanking either side of the stand are flagpoles bearing national, state, province, and tribal flags.

Dance floors are leveled areas of grass, sawdust, packed earth, or, as in the case of the Blackfeet, high-tech astro turf, which takes five people three days to nail down. Each surface has good and bad qualities, with grass being the most favored by dancers and sawdust the least favored. "Sawdust is like trying to dance in sand; there is no firm footing from which to push off. It clings to furs and fringe, gets everywhere," said Arnold Boss Calf Ribs, a Blackfeet traditional dancer. "It's still dusty and it can be so deep I wonder if I'm dancing on someone's head," he joked.

Tipis make an Indian camp and capture the imagination. The magic of walking at night and seeing these structures glowing gold from fires within warms the heart. Woodsmoke drifts through the air tickling the nose, shadows playing on canvas walls attract the eyes, occasional laughter and happy voices punctuate silence, as families and friends settle down. This world is at peace, and tipis stand guard providing home and haven.

Painted designs on tipis have great spiritual significance within tribal boundaries. Designs are not painted arbitrarily as some non-Indians are wont to do in recent years. The designs are a distinct part of spiritual culture. Men went on vision quests to high mountain peaks or lonely buttes to receive these designs. A spirit would show how to paint them. The design became "medicine" with protective properties for his family and tribe. Each painted tipi has a certain set of instructions that the owners must observe. A design must be given in a ceremony.

Woody Kipp
Grass Dancer
Blackfeet

Water, so essential to our lives, creates a gathering point at powwows. Often grounds have faucets fed from wells spaced around the area. Just as often only one or two supply entire camps. Kids surround them on hot days, filling water balloons and squirt guns. Others wash hair, rinse clothes, or fill containers for evening coffee. These frequently visited waterholes turn into wallows around which one walks gingerly to avoid mud.

Camps along rivers or streams have swimming holes that draw people on hot days. It's not uncommon to see men, women, children, horses and dogs all splashing together in the Little Big Hole River at Crow Agency, or swimming at Crazy Head Lakes near Lame Deer, Montana. What nature

BELOW: A small arbor offers shade for one family and their guests at Crow Fair.
FACING PAGE: Painted designs of Blackfeet tipis.

doesn't provide, man will. Irrigation ditches provide relief in Arlee. Swarms of kids follow dust-control trucks watering down roads, arenas, and an occasional kid, at powwows everywhere.

Modern facilities are replacing those infamous dilapitated outhouses. Luxury accommodations treat visitors to showers on the grounds. Quality rest rooms feature flush toilets (if kids haven't tried to drown a roll of paper). Wooden privies give way to "plastic potties" with pumpable chemical tanks.

All camps have medical and first aid available on the grounds. Staffed by Indian Health Services or private paramedics, facilities quickly handle medical emergencies.

Regular tribal police and special deputies provide security. Each camp has a central command post and foot patrols circulate vigilantly. Officers are recognized by their uniforms, badges, and long-handled flashlights. Much like the dog soldiers of years ago they insure that the camp behaves in a proper manner.

All powwows, being family events, forbid the use of drugs and alcohol, which are not allowed through the gate. Campers under the influence are firmly asked to leave by both their peers and police. "It's okay to have a good time, but if you are drinking you are not wanted here" and "VIOLATORS WILL BE FINED AND JAILED" are common warnings that permeate powwows.

In recent years, tribes and urban Indian organizations have used traditional values and customs as effective tools in combating alcohol and drug abuse. As the showcase of Indian cultural expression, the powwow has led the way in discouraging alcohol and drug use.

In the past, northern camps were messy and frequently littered. Tribes oganized work parties of children to clean up after the event. Today committees are conscious of the necessity to encourage effective sanitation. Garbage bags are handed out

FACING PAGE, TOP: *Walking around the encampment is part of enjoying powwow.*
BOTTOM: *The author, with camera, visits with a Blackfeet friend, Phillip Dog Gun. Kurt Wilson photo*
THIS PAGE, TOP LEFT: *Blackfeet tipi.*
RIGHT: *The international flavor of powwow on Rocky Boy's Reservation.*
BOTTOM LEFT: *Powwow is the time for meeting new friends and visiting with old ones.*
RIGHT: *Indian flags at sunset.*

A woman in traditional buckskin dress, carrying fry bread, pauses for the camera.

along with rations. Filled containers are emptied daily. Instead of looking trashed out on tear-down day, many camps are dotted with neat piles of tightly tied bags.

No one has found an effective method for control of ever-present insects. They like to powwow too.

Camp Activities

Visiting entails the majority of camp activity. "Come sit, have a cup of coffee," "Here, grab a plate and eat," "Come to our camp so we can talk," are greetings to old friends and new acquaintances alike. Mornings, afternoons, evenings, and late nights after dance sessions friends and families gather around the campfire or the Coleman stove, sharing coffee, tea, and stories. This time becomes "catch up time" when relatives find out what's going on in the distant reaches of their family tree. Who's married, who's divorced, what children were born, who died, facts and fantasies trickle forth to everyone's interest.

Many tribes distribute "rations" to their campers. The old custom of feeding your guests carries on in this manner or in the previously discussed feeds. Hosts place sacks of groceries outside the door of all tents, tipis, and RV's. These sacks contain staples of meat, coffee, bread, and vegetables. Rations can be distributed by asking guests to come and pick them up from a centrally parked truck.

Guests who refuse food are considered impolite. When offered food, they must eat. Among all cultures, eating together links people and forms bonds. The custom of feeding in the powwow world serves to strengthen inter-tribal ties and relationships.

"Originally, when there was a powwow, food was prepared and all visitors were invited to take meals with various families. This tradition continues today. It is very important to the powwow and not too much emphasis can be given this part at encampments," commented Blackfeet artist Leon Rattler. "At every powwow we attended this summer, we would be invited to different family camps for breakfast, lunch, dinner, and supper. Many times we did not dare to eat too much in one place because another family had invited us to the same meal. Sometimes we would be invited to eat at three or four camps," Debbie Rattler, Leon's wife added.

"One of the best ways to understand a people is to know what makes them laugh," writes Vine Deloria, Jr., a Sioux, in *Custer Died for Your Sins*. "Indian people are exactly opposite of the popular stereotype. Indians have found a humorous side of nearly every problem and experience of life." In a chapter on Indian humor Deloria quotes Indian one-liners like: "Custer was well dressed, he wore an Arrow shirt."

When asked why Indians were the first people on this continent, according to Deloria, the Pueblo artist Popovi Da replied, "We had reservations." Another story goes that, an Indian asked by an anthropologist on what Indians called America before the arrival of the whiteman, answered simply, "Ours."

When I asked my Oklahoma-born friend Dennis Hanna, "What tribe are you?" he replied, "I'm not. I'm just one person." Dennis, an Apache, added that non-Indians in Oklahoma are called "tourists."

Indians sometimes joke differently with strangers than with friends. They try to put the newcomer on edge, to increase anxiety knowing the person is already nervous. They will appear unfriendly and uncooperative. When that person is thoroughly flustered they will break into a wide grin, and with twinkling eyes, say, "I jokes," in a manner similiar to "gotcha!"

Indian humor, as it relates to the non-Indian, is a testing of that person. We try to create a nervousness, to see if that other person will flinch. That testing is based on our old tradition of the coup stick. To be brave enough to strike the enemy and not kill him.

Kip White Cloud

"Indian masses" may take place in the arbor on Sunday mornings. Catholicism is strong on many reservations, and clerics now realize that incorporating native customs into their services increases attendance and does nothing to diminish the respect extended towards the Creator. Priests wear special vestments with Indian motifs. Processionals led by elders in buckskins and war bonnets attract the faithful. Ceremonies conducted in native tongues allow traditions to merge. Indians can remain Indian while embracing Christianity if they so choose.

Indian camps are not Indian without horses. In most camps, they are everywhere. Decorated in beaded harnesses, they color parades. Kids ride around the grounds three up, and bareback. Impromptu races kick up dust and commotion at the edge of camp. Chased by its owner, an occasional loose horse furnishes afternoon excitement as it bounds among tents and tourists. Whinnies and snorts break the night silence.

Sleeping is secondary to other activities at powwows, participants fitting it in as necessary or when a break in the events allows. With all the dancing, gambling, and visiting, the blackness of night gives way to the pink glow of sunrise before tired people find their pillows. Nights on the plains can be cold and days hot. Differences of 40 and 50 degrees are not uncommon. The sleeper who piles the blankets on at 6 a.m., wakes to an oppressive heat at 10 a.m., unable to sleep. "Might as well go visit, can't sleep anyway. I'll catch a nap later."

Effectively cutting into sleep due to late-night occurrence is "the 49." This social dance employs the same step as the round dance, but takes place when the regular dance sessions have ended. Participants gather at a secluded spot, bringing out a drum; if one is not available, a car hood or cardboard box will substitute quite well. Quality of sound is not essential. Songs for a "49" consist of a combination of vocables and English words and generally have romance as a theme. Partners "share blankets" holding each other close, singles look to pair up or "snag." Camaraderie is the key element. People come together to be close, to share good feelings with each other.

Many stories exist as to how this dance got its name. One says a group of Indians working at a wild west show kept hearing a carnival barker eliciting people to, "Come see the 49 [1849] cancan girls, see the 49ers dance." Not to be outdone, these Indian performers initiated their own 49 dance. Another tells that either 49 of 50 warriors were slain or returned from battle and the dance is named in their honor.

This dance usually involves teens or young adults as they have the stamina to "49" all night long, although older married couples will join in rejuvenating themselves under star-filled skies to popular songs and warm blankets. Songs like:
When you hear the whistle blow,
I must go away.
Wey, Hey Ya, Hey Ya.
I will see you again next summertime,
Crow Indian Fair and Rodeo!
Wey, Hey Ya, Hey Ya.
Oh yes, I love you, honey dear.
I don't care if you've been married 15 times,
I'll get you yet!
I miss my sweetheart,
I miss my sweetheart,
She's in jail!
Wey, Hey Ya, Hey Ya!

Douglas Standing Rock catches a nap during a dance competition.

Gigi Yazzie and her family enjoying powwow.

Cultural Identity

Powwows give a sense of tribal cohesion and racial identification.

The powwow helps Indian people to take pride in themselves as individuals, family and tribal members, and as a race. "The powwow is in a state of flux due to the vast number of people who are returning to their tribal cultures in search of a positive identity. Old ways are being remembered and taught to young tribal members. This dance represents something sacred and infinitely communal," Woody Kipp wrote in response to a question about the meaning of powwows. "As powwow dancers search ever deeper into their own culture for dance styles and outfits that are authentic, they become aware that the meaning of life is represented by the dancing circle of their people. They become aware of their place and responsibilities within their nations. They become aware they are dancing for a reason."

The powwow has increased our nationalism, our tribal identities, and our identities as native North Americans. I hear people say, "Why do you Indians fight so hard for treaty rights, you already fought for your land?" Signs say, "Spear an Indian, save a fish" or "Indian reservations are totalitarian dictatorships." These people don't realize, this is our homeland. Non-Indians have an "old country" they can return to. A homeland to their language and customs. This is our old coun-

102

No matter what color you are, it's the feeling in the heart that counts. That feeling overcomes any nationality. Indian people pray for all people—so that they see another day. Indian life is tough, it's hard. I believe I can do anything in this world if I put my mind to it, if I put my heart into it. I get up in the morning, I wash my face like everyone else. I pray to the same Creator. I don't have to go into a building to find the Creator. That comes from my Indian heritage.

Kip White Cloud, Traditional Dancer
Sioux

try. We have no place else to go. Why should we give it up?

Boye Ladd
Fancy and Exhibition Dancer
Winnebago

I was born in California and returned to the Blackfeet Reservation in my twenties. There's no jobs here. I've accepted Montana as a "wilderness state." I miss things from the city and visit there occasionally, though I'll take the reservation anytime. I love the mountains, trees, streams, and fresh air. I hunt, fish, and breathe. The city is scary. Even with no money I better stay right here and raise my family right. Introduce them to the powwow.

James Watt
Traditional Dancer
Blackfeet

Indian culture is getting stronger, there will always be Indians.

Kip White Cloud
Traditional Dancer
Sioux

Indian people were tired of always trying to be white. We were unhappy, lost. Powwows show us we have our own life, beliefs, and culture. We learn that we are alike as Indians, our beliefs are the same. This makes us closer, we learn from one another. We each can do something good. Powwows show us we are what we are. We are all people.

Phillip Paul
Singer and Traditional Dancer
Flathead

Families and individuals gain pride and honor from participating in powwows. "Indians today are starting to identify with what was once and still is uniquely theirs. Assimilation tried to suppress our traditional ways. By starting at an early age, younger Indians are learning the value of traditional education and life," commented Leon Rattler. "Growing up with these values will insure that future generations continue to identify as Indian. The powwow is the main showcase of our culture, and the participants fuel regrowth and awareness," he added.

George Horse Capture, curator of the Buffalo Bill Historical Center in Cody, Wyoming, pointed out, "the dances of the powwow are an important competitive medium for our young people, as well as being a 'sport' and a way of showing their capabilities and athletic talents." He noted that in the "buffalo days energetic young men went off to war to demonstrate their prowess and abilities. Returning home, they achieved honor, status, and a place in their world."

Buffalo hunts and intertribal warring have gone by the wayside. Indian reservations, located in isolated rural areas, with little money, have difficulty nurturing conventional professional athletes or cultural performers. "In our world there are two areas where one can compete to earn honor and prestige. One is rodeo, the other is the powwow," added Horse Capture.

Serious participants on the circuit may attend as many as forty powwows a season. This sub-group gains reputations for their abilities and sponsoring organizations appreciate their attendance. Many dancers expend as much energy and commitment to the "sport of powwow dancing" as the warriors of pre-reservation days. They are superstars of the circuits and travel wide areas to compete with each other.

Champions are champions, both on and off the floor. Every one of these champions has a

Joe Arlee, a Flathead, is a traditional dancer.

...a rivalry comes along. The spirits are strong. Like Johnny [Whitecloud] and Gordon [Lasley]. North against South. I never saw anything more powerful than when those guys danced. You knew which steps, which moves belonged to who. You'd catch a step and say, "There's a new one," or Johnny would do the splits, a back flip, or a cartwheel and blow everyone's mind.

Boye Ladd, Fancy Dancer
Winnebago

certain aura, a certain personality. They get along great with people, they give, they share.
Boye Ladd

Beginning in the late 1940s and early '50s, picking up momentum by the mid 1960s, a transformation of tremendous magnitude occurred in "Indian Country." Indian people recognized themselves and renewed their pride in being Indian. The modern proliferation of powwows is the strongest evidence of this native cultural renaissance.

We should tap the wealth of knowledge in our elders and use what they give us. They are a great resource and we should use them more. I thank my grandfather Leon Spotted Bull for who I am. Ever since I was little my grandparents taught me the do's and dont's. I was raised in their image. I lived with them since I was one day old.

Kip White Cloud

Traditional values regained their prominence in native societies. Elders re-emerged as respected tribal resources and are sought out for their wisdom. Old ways are taught once again. Parents and teachers are encouraged to instruct students in native histories, customs, crafts, and languages.

Sometimes there is only one dancer in the family. It's up to him to go to powwows and have a good time. It's his job as a dancer to introduce the powwow to his family. They may not like it right then. Then he has to back up and let them take it when they are ready.

James Watt

The values I would pass along are the values of friendship and the values of our elders and

106

FACING PAGE TOP: Harriet Standing Rock's daughter sports a scarf in the traditional manner.
BOTTOM: Ron Walsey shows off a modern version of a Mandan-style headdress.
CLOCKWISE FROM TOP LEFT:
John Peter Paul in traditional Flathead dress.
Cheyenne dancer Phillip Whiteman, Jr.
Traditional Pawnee face paint.
Blackfeet grass dancer Phillip Dog Gun.
Cecile Horn, a Blackfeet elder.
Smile from a young Crow girl.
Pacific coastal-style woven hat.

Today there is a forty and over dance for "old" fancy dancers who went traditional. What about us fancy dancers who haven't switched? I'm an old timer, I stay with my footwork, can't really do acrobatics. What is dance anyway but footwork? Dance is telling a story, your exploits, what you saw in battle, different things you did. You step, you balance, you crouch. It's what you do in dance.

Boye Ladd, Fancy Dancer
Winnebago

Left: A Umatilla woman's traditional dress and beaded hat.
Facing page: Kip White Cloud in his Sioux traditional outfit.

their wisdom. Remember who you are. You cannot be something you are not. Lose that perspective and you lose your life, as an Indian, as a white man, as a person.

Kip White Cloud

Cross-Cultural Relations

Increasingly, non-Indians visit powwows and experience the Indian world. They see entire families involved in a rich manifestation of culture. Old stereotypes peel away, replaced by appreciation of this continent's native peoples. Indian people welcome these guests knowing this new understanding fosters harmony and goodwill.

When non-Indians say we are losing our culture, I say they don't know what they are talking about. They haven't been to our celebrations. Look out there! See those dancers, see those kids, hear those drums, those songs. They should have enough respect not to open their mouths before they open their eyes and

ears. That stereotype is the wrong image of Indians.

Tony Brown
Fancy and Hoop Dancer
Oneida-Sioux-Flathead

If non-Indians learned more about us, we could get along better and learn from each other.

Phillip Paul

The powwow helps us learn about each other, to respect customs and ways. Elders teach, "Don't be something you're not, and respect others' lives, customs, and areas." It's the same with powwow circles. At my home circle I have my rights. When I visit the Flathead or the Blackfeet in Montana I come to their circle. "When in Rome, do as the Romans." When in Sioux country do as the Sioux. My customs stay at home, they don't come into another's circle. Some dance circles go clockwise, some counter-clockwise, I go with the flow.

Boye Ladd

Improved relations between Indians and whites are coming about. Whites are coming to us for our values. They are enjoying the powwow and seeing Indian people as they really are. This expression of culture has opened us up to each other.

Kip White Cloud

Indian people are the most loving people there are. Come to a powwow, the place where all nationalities, all races are accepted.

Tony Brown

The Powwow Experience

"All you dancers! All you dancers! Start getting ready. It's powwow time. Grand Entry at one o'clock. Drum roll call in fifteen minutes. Let's get over to the arbor and get set up." The buckskin-attired emcee urges participants to finish lunch, or in the case of 49ers, a late breakfast. The sun shines directly overhead, hinting of the heat to come at North American Indian Days on the Blackfeet reservation.

"Singers, let's start making your way over to the arbor. Host drum duties this afternoon will be handled by Black Lodge. Kenny Scabby Robe, you are wanted at your drum, your boys are missing you, they say they are still hungry." Earl Old Person makes a joke directed at Black Lodge's lead singer. Kenny's teenage sons, cousins, and friends make up this popular drum group. Dancers, you are to line up at the east entrance of the arbor. Have your numbers visible, they will be taken this afternoon. You will get Grand Entry points. Let's go! *Buks-sa-put!* Let's go!" Blackfeet intermingles with "English" as Earl exhorts everyone to get ready. "Grand Entry promptly at one o' clock. No Indian time."

I don't think we'll ever see an end to the pow-wow like nearly happened in the old days. As long as there are Indians living there is gonna be powwows. It just gives me a good feeling. I like to watch the dancers and I like to participate. It's fun.

Joe Sam Scabby Robe
Grass Dancer and Singer
Blackfeet

Many groups start setting up. Bass drums with rawhide heads sit on blankets or hang suspended from carved wooden supports. Black speaker horns ring the arbor roof, cabinets stand like mini-monoliths on the dance floor. The whines, whistles and squawks of the public address system compete with booming drums as both are tightened and tuned.

"It's time for drum roll call. Black Lodge, are you there?" Boom, boom, boom, comes the reply as the singers indicate their readiness by striking the drum.

"Starr School, are you there?" Boom, boom, boom, another reply. "Eagle Whistles, how about you?" A rumble answers his question. "Mandaree… Chiniki Lake… Heart Butte… Teton Ramblers… Kicking Woman… Young Grey Horse… Northern Cheyenne… Parker… Chief Cliff… Old Agency… Stoney Park… All Nations… Mesquakie Bear Singers." The drums ringing the arbor all respond to the call.

At a powwow we are celebrating, we are giving thanks. People come from all over to make themselves feel good. That's what it's all about. Different people coming together and welcoming each other. It's not a place to be mad, or sad. It is a place to put aside those feelings and be happy, to enjoy life and who you are.

Tony Brown
Fancy and Exhibition Dancer
Oneida-Sioux-Flathead

"Dancers, line up! Men's traditional first. Followed by men's fancy, then grass. Then women's traditional, fancy, then jingle dress. You kids follow behind the adults in the same categories." The dancers who have been milling around, visiting with each other, adjusting outfits, shuffle into rough lines. Flag bearers move to the head of the parade.

"Ho Kay folks, it's Grand Entry time. Ah Ho! Black Lodge take it away, you'll be followed by Kicking Woman for the first intertribal."

Phillip Dog Gun proudly holds high America's red, white and blue flag. Walter Bull bears the red maple leaf of Canada, while John Grounds carries the eagle-feathered Indian flag. It takes over a half an hour to get all 900 dancers onto the floor. Joe Bear Medicine asks the Creator's blessing for all those present. Hats are removed and heads bow while everyone adds his own thoughts and feelings to the Blackfeet words. The moment of silence over everyone is ready to "cut loose on their first intertribal."

When the Grand Entry is over and all the dancers are in, this feeling comes over me. I know that I am part of a world that belongs to myself, my family, and friends that have been made in this sacred circle. No one can come and take it away.

Dana Runs Above
Jingle Dress Dancer
Assiniboine

"Chief Cliff, you're on deck for an intertribal. Give 'em a good one. Take it away. Remember only four starts, four pushups. There are 22 drums here today and we want to get all the way 'round the arbor before our first special. Videl Stump, your group is up next."

The powwow today is changing, it's become bigger and better and there are more of them. There's lots of people getting interested in powwows now. When I started dancing I saw people who I haven't seen again 'til now. They're all coming back. That is the good part for me, seeing all my friends participating and enjoying themselves again.

Joe Sam Scabby Robe

Tim White Eyes carrying the Indian flag for grand entry.

If you compare dance styles and costuming, even footwork, to what existed thirty or forty years ago, there's no comparison. You can't match the kind of costuming today to what existed in the Fifties, Sixties and early Seventies. There's thousands of dollars and countless hours in the costumes, and good dancers practice and train constantly. All the good singing groups have recorded tapes available to train to. What we've got today is the best.

Boye Ladd, Fancy Dancer
Winnebago

114

Powwowing to me is real important. It's part of me. I was 19 when I first got into it. A time in my life when it was something to do besides drugs and alcohol. It got me into being physical, to dance out things I'd see.
As I walk in this world, I see things that I don't really like. I don't know where they come from nor where they go. They're there. Dancing purifies me, cleans me. I sweat them out. The dance song makes me feel good. I move in rhythm to it. I feel that my family's gonna be okay, the future's gonna be okay. I see my kids, my family, my relations all dancing in the powwow. I am happy.

James Watt
Traditional Dancer
Blackfeet

"Clear the arbor. Clear the arbor. We have a special coming up."

The dancers return to their seats or head to the concessions for a cool drink. "Bearhead Swaney, please report to the announcer's stand, we need you to say just a few words. If you *can,* I jokes." Bearhead, a Flathead activist, is known for his eloquence. "We have a child up here who says her parents are lost. If anyone recognizes this little girl please come and get her. Okay, Young Grey Horse, will you do the honors for the White Grass family giveaway? Everybody please rise."

To me the powwow opens up Indian people to the spirit of our traditions. It allows us to determine what is real and what is not.
It expands our world as Indians. Teaches us what is spiritual and what is material. The real interpretation of powwow is to give.
Not giving to get something back, but giving just to give. Somewhere, somehow it always balances out and that giving comes back

around. That is a big part of the powwow world.

Boye Ladd, Fancy and Exhibition Dancer
Winnebago

"Would Orlando Calling Last please come and receive a gift from the White Grass family? The family asks that Steve Small Salmon come up and receive a gift. Charles Tailfeathers! The family calls Charles Tailfeathers to come receive a gift. Wayne and Thelma Bear Medicine, you are asked to receive this Pendleton blanket and shake hands with the family for singing the honor song. Would four elderly visitors come receive gifts…" People called come forward to receive blankets, food, cloth and money. They shake hands with a long line of family members, before returning to their place in the arbor.

"Ladies and gentlemen, that concludes the afternoon dance session.

"Tonight's Grand Entry will be at seven o'clock. It's time for dinner break. Drum roll call at six thirty. All visitors are invited to a feast at the Bull Child camp in honor of Percy and Bobby."

Singers fold their chairs and lean them next to the drum. Dancers remove headdresses and bustles, returning to camp to eat, rest and make repairs on their outfits. Many will change shirts and beadwork, altering their looks so as to attract the judges' eyes in the evening session.

To a certain extent powwow dancers can be seen as modern-day warriors. Spirit against spirit. Cree against Sioux, or whatever. When they dance against each other, it looks good—there's a tribal style, their own way. All trying to outdo each other.

Boye Ladd

"Ah Ho! I'm back. I'm fed and I'm ready to go. Get ready for the seven o'clock Grand Entry." Preparation for the evening's contests replaces the quiet relaxed atmosphere that had settled over camp during dinner. Dancers apply fresh face paint, comb out headdresses, wrap strained knees, and pad moccasins. "Tonight we have the finals in the adult categories. We'll see who is going to walk off with the big money.

"Make sure everything is tied tight. The judges say you will be disqualified if you drop part of your outfit."

After dancing four days at a powwow, I feel it. My joints are sore and I feel older than I really am. Then I see this old guy out there dancing. I think, "I'm still young." I pull strength from the other people. I'm out there by myself, me and the Creator. I'm dancing with the drum and everybody around me is supporting me or else they wouldn't be there. They reinforce me, give me life. They share themselves.

James Watt

The colorful Grand Entry again begins the evening session. A Veterans of Foreign Wars color guard, wearing war bonnets with uniforms, retires the colors. A series of intertribals thoroughly warms the dancers in the late afternoon heat. The setting sun signals it's time to "run off the contests." Bearhead Swaney, of Salish (Flathead) descent, alternates with Blackfeet Chief Earl Old Person on the microphone, sharing announcing duties. "I hear it gets so hot that the Blackfeet are going to hire a rainmaker. Yeah, they're going to get a white man from Cut Bank [east of the Blackfeet reservation] to come to Browning and wash his car," he jokes. Flatheads and Blackfeet were traditional antagonists and a friendly rivalry continues to this day.

"It's contest time. All you fancy dancers, seventeen and over, when I call your number, get out

on the floor. Judges, are you ready? Number 801." Chico Her Many Horses, a Sioux from South Dakota, steps out shaking his bustles, checking their fit.

"Number 810." Luke Whiteman, the local champion, takes his place in the circle.

"Number 813." Gary Comes At Night, another Blackfeet, makes his way forward.

"Number 817." Eric George, a young seventeen-year-old Yakima from Washington, makes the finals with seasoned adults.

"Number 821... number 836... number 840..." The list goes on until twelve finalists circle the arbor. "Cathedral Lake Singers, give us the Shake. Southern Drum, give us a Fast and Fancy. Castle Rock Singers, you got the Crow Hop." The contestants know those three songs will completely exhaust them and determine the winners.

Most everybody trains today, you've got to work out, to run, build your strength, your

If you look back to the beginnings of powwows, you'll see respect for warriors. What they learned or experienced in battle was brought out in dance-story form. That respect today is directed towards the veterans of our armed services. Patriotism is a big part of powwows. We are basically respecting love. Love of freedom, love of country, love of family. How can you teach love without some reference point…teaching war, and respect for warriors?

Boye Ladd, Fancy Dancer
Winnebago

118

timing. There are more good dancers today than ever. Dancers all have their own little secrets for keeping in shape and doing their best.

Boye Ladd

I don't really train or practice as a dancer. I dance to feel good about myself. I give it a hundred and twenty percent. When I do that, I am good. I feel my feet float over the dance floor. I am light. My moves come easy. I fly with the song, my spirit soars to the sky.

Tony Brown

Rivalries can exist between good dancers. Like Gordon Lasley and Johnny White Cloud. North against south. Their spirits are strong. I never saw anything more powerful than when those guys danced. You knew which steps, which moves belonged to whom. You'd catch a step and say, "There's a new one," or Johnny would do the splits, a backflip, then stop on a cartwheel and blow everyone's mind.

Boye Ladd

"Thank you, dancers; thank you, singers. Clear the arbor. We have had a request for a round dance. Haystack Ramblers, give us a round dance. Everybody get out there. You do not have to be in costume to dance the round dance. You do not have to be an Indian. Just get out there, join in. Ah Ho, let's go! You dancers go to the audience and bring some people out to join in the circle. Ah eee Yah!" The arbor fills with costumed dancers, and spectators in street clothes. Women wear shawls warding off the evening coolness. Children start a line in a reverse direction, giggling and shaking hands with the line in front. Everybody gets out there.

When I grew up there were some kids dancing but there wasn't that many. Lots of them didn't stick with it. Now it's good to see eighty tiny tots out there. To see forty Junior Boys or Girls in each division. It makes me feel good to see that.

Joe Sam Scabby Robe

"Thank you, everybody. Now that you are warmed up let's have another intertribal. Whose turn is it in the rotation?" A drum ruffle and a loud cough on the P.A. from Wade Baker indicate it's Eagle Whistles' turn. "Take it away, Eagle Whistles!" The group launches into a slow- to medium-paced "favorite" that gets everyone dancing. Traditionals congregate close to the singers, forming an aisle to the drum, in which dancers take their turn "soloing." Byron Heavy Runner blows his whistle honoring the drum. "We have a whistle on the drum!" The song is sung through again. The pace picks up. The dancers seem to be in a trance. Cleveland High Bull comes forward and blows his whistle. "We have another whistle on the drum!"

Again the song is sung. Men and women fancy dancers spin wildly outside the traditionals. Grass and jingle dancers join the melee—

119

I used to have negative feelings towards jealousies I encountered on the powwow circuit. Then I realized without jealousies and competiveness we wouldn't have survived 'til today. It's that competition between tribes that instills pride in our people and perpetuates our customs and traditions. The powwow plays a big part in this tribal spirit. We are Ojibwa, Ponca, Cheyenne, Crow or Cree first. We are nations within a nation. The powwow is a "Gathering of Nations."

Boye Ladd, Fancy Dancer
Winnebago

twisting, bobbing, gyrating, and jingling. The song, now fast and furious, transports the dancers and they float free. Yesterday's anguish, today's worries, and tomorrow's troubles do not exist. There is only now, this rapturous, golden moment. The Creator is kind. Life is good. All is well. Twenty exhausting minutes later the song ends and everyone rests.

> *It's me and the Creator. I don't know how to explain it. He knows what I'm feeling inside. He encourages me to dance good for Him all the time. He encourages me to try better than I did last year. We're always trying to please the Creator. I get better as a person every day I get better as a powwow dancer. When we are dancing we have a relationship with the Creator. We have a relationship with the drum. I see this.*
>
> James Watt

"Time for an exhibition dance, folks. Tony Brown, are you ready?" Tony Brown performs a crowd-pleasing hoop dance. In his finale he encircles himself with a globe of twenty hoops and in a magical instant they fall to his feet. Drum beats, bell ringing, and hand clapping indicate the audience's appreciation as Tony leaves the dance floor.

"Ladies and gentlemen, we have a dance-off in Men's Traditional. Would numbers 915, 937 and 945 get out there?" Three dancers stride confidently into the arena. One dancer's paint divides his face—half black, the other white—giving him an intimidating appearance. Another's loose fringe and feathers create a shimmering effect as he walks, accentuating every movement. The third's bright beaded designs complement the intricate featherwork of his bustles, catching the eye. These dancers know they are dancing for the money. Good sports,

120

*Traditional dancers. Ken Shane, wearing traditional Crow
hair style, faces the camera.*

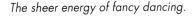
The sheer energy of fancy dancing.

they shake each other's hands and limber up, stretching, shaking and bending their bodies while the judges confer on which drum group to use for the contest finale.

I like both traditional powwows and money powwows. But in this day and age we need money to survive. It's not just feeding horses anymore. You have to take care of your individual needs, keep your vehicle running, put gas in the tank, food in your belly. We gotta keep up with the times. It takes money to survive in the powwow world.

Tony Brown

The cost of attending powwows has really risen. Inflation. Today filling up a van costs fifty bucks. Dancers have to pay four to five hundred dollars for bustle sets, two to three hundred for headdresses. Beadwork can run into thousands. A person really has to be dedicated to be involved.

Boye Ladd

Powwows today are different than when I was a boy. We used to dance for a money prize then but it was a lower amount. There was less pressure to win, and more fun. Today's powwows have to have large amounts of money to attract good dancers and singers. Money has changed the old ways.

Kip White Cloud
Traditional Dancer
Sioux

"Badlands has been selected to sing a Sneak Up, and Pat Kennedy's group, Starr School, sing the slow war dance. Okay, dancers, here we go. This is a dance-off for one, two, three."
Seymour Eagle Speaker and Billy Runs

Above take turns leading Badlands during the Sneak Up. The song enables the dancers to show off their best moves, each crouching low to the ground searching for the enemy, then "sneaking up" with soft, deliberate steps and surprising him. Breaking into a victory dance, they whoop and holler dancing wildly in celebration of their "successful encounter."

Next comes the slow war dance and each contestant demonstrates his character and style. Head and eyes dart from place to place, ever vigilant. Shoulders shake feathers and fringe. Proud chests display beadwork and breastplates. Arms and hands hold shield and tomahawk ready. Hips bend and twist, bustles dip and flow. Dancers step backward, forward, and in circles. Feet step hard, then soft, ringing bells in age-old rhythms.

"You're looking good, looking good. Let's hear it for these dancers. They are real champions. They know how to show us some great dancing. Ah Ho!" The song ends and each dancer stops with a flourish exactly on beat. "It's going to be hard for the judges to decide." The dancers line up and ballots are marked carefully. Shaking hands and complementing each other, they return to their families to await the results.

"Okay, the ballots have been tabulated and we have the contest results. In the twelve and under, Junior Girls Jingle Dress your third place winner is… Your second place winner is… Your First Place winner is…"

Excited children run forward laughing and smiling, their braids flying behind them, their feet off the ground. They receive their money from the arena director, shake hands with officials and contestants, and line up nervously fidgeting while other winners are announced.

"Your third place winner in Men's Traditional is number 937, Junior Two Teeth, a Cree from Helena, Montana. Your second place winner, number 915, Bob Brave Rock, a member of the Blood tribe from Cardston, Alberta, Canada. And your first place winner, a drum roll please, an Assiniboine from Hays, Montana, winning fifteen hundred dollars, number 9-4-5, Timothy Eashappie, Sr.! Congratulations, Tim!

"All you dancers, this Victory Dance is for you. Maynard Kicking Woman, you're on. Sing it sweet for these champion dancers. Once around the arbor, then everyone join in for "Home Sweet Home." Chief Cliff Singers, you have the honors on that one. Good night, everybody. We'll see you next year."

I love powwows. I can sit and listen to the songs, bells and drumming for the rest of my life. It's a different world to be a part of. The feeling of being part of it, the whole scene, singing and dancing, being Indian, is an extraordinary feeling.

Dana Runs Above

I go to the powwow because I want to enjoy the powwow spirit, I want to enjoy the music, live for the moment when I hit that one song…then I am one with the Creator.

Boye Ladd

Glossary

Announcers, Masters of Ceremonies—All powwows have these. They keep the event going, announcing events, explaining exhibition dances, telling jokes, calling for lost parents, seeking owners for lost items.

Arena Directors—usually honored dancers who keep track of drum order and dance contests; they help coordinate contest events.

Arbor—the dance circle surrounded by bleachers and overhead shade, usually tree boughs on a framework. The announcer's stand is usually to the west, and entries are on the four points of the compass. Drum locations are marked with numbers.

Contest Dances—Categories are divided by age (ranging from tiny tots to golden age or over 65), gender, and dance style. Categories include:

Men's Fancy Dance—Divisions are Young Boys, Teens, Senior Men. This dance style is characterized by bright, colorful, flashy outfits decorated with beadwork and brilliant-hued hackle feather bustles. Dancers use intricate, fast and acrobatic motions. Men wear knee bells for keeping time.

Women's Fancy Dance—Women's outfits replace bustles with fancy, embroidered shawls with long fringe to accentuate movement. The women don't wear bells.

Men's and Women's Traditional—Dancers wear natural outfits, with leather the predominant material, with bead colors and patterns traditionally based. Men wear haw and eagle feather bustles and bone breastplates. Women wear beaded buckskin dresses.

    The traditional dancer is proud and deliberate. The male dancer throws his chest out and bends low, carefully moving his head and body. Female dancers carry themselves with dignity and grace. Their subtle and precise dance steps cause their dresses' long buckskin fringe to sway in gentle harmony with their bodies.

Grass Dance—an alternative male style with origins in the Plains states. Dancers wear brightly colored yarn fringe on their outfits. They move their hips, arms and shoulders, rocking and shaking their bodies with strenuous movements, and executing intricate footwork.

Jingle Dress—a women's dance style named after the large tin cone "jingles" sewn in line or chevron patterns on form-fitting, movement-restricting dresses.

Dance types

Exhibition Dance—usually a solo or limited-group performances, such as the Hoop Dance, tribal cultural dances from the Southwest, Northwest Coast or East Coast. Sometimes a team or dance-style exhibition.

49—Takes place on the fringes of the camp when the formal dance is over. Requirements are a good blanket to share with your partner and stamina to last till the sun comes up.

Honor Dance—a special dance, sung to honor a person or event. Participants usually are family members, and friends and dancers circle the arbor.

Intertribals—include all dance styles in an everyone-dance situation, all ages and genders. The announcer will usually say, "Let's everyone dance, all you dancers get out there."

Owl Dance—similar to a round dance but with partners, and women ask men to dance.

Round Dance—a two-step danced in a circles, a social dance with all invited: Indian and non-Indian, costumed or not.

Drum—see Singer/Drum Groups.

Fry Bread—bread dough fried in hot fat and served with honey and butter; powerfully fattening and delicious. The recipe varies.

Grand Entry—the parade of dancers that leads off each session of the powwow. Sometimes contestants' numbers are recorded and they receive points for participation.

Giveaway—distribution of goods by a family to friends, relatives and visitors in honor of a person or event, for example to memorialize someone's death, for a naming ceremony or an adoption. Goods range from blankets to foodstuffs to horses covered in money. The giveaway is preceded by an Honor Song.

Indian Taco—Fry bread served with chili, cheese, tomatoes and onions. Good stuff!

Indian Flag—a staff, spiritual in nature, covered in fur and hung with eagle feathers, which represents Indian-ness and/or a tribe, carried with honor by a veteran in the opening ceremonies.

Indian Time—the time all powwows run on. Schedules are set, but are flexible, and attempts are made to adhere to them strictly but…due to the informal nature of large gatherings, times are approximate. Things start when they start and end when they end.

Powwow Circuit—similar to a rodeo circuit, and entire families travel them from Memorial Day to Labor Day. Basic divisions are the Northern Circuit in the Plains states, and the Southern Circuit centered in Oklahoma. One dancer has identified 16 regional circuits in the U.S. and Canada. People traveling the circuit consist of dancers, singers, gamblers, rodeo riders, announcers and concessionaires. The circuit can be addictive, and is a wonderful opportunity to meet people and learn.

Singer/Drum Groups—The music of the powwow circuit, each usually include five to 10 members (and sometimes entire families), with a lead singer and others who can "second" (repeat the lead line with melody on a different or similar key). Dancers key their movements to the melody of the song, their footwork keeping time to the drumbeat. Singers have a variety of song styles they offer in order to allow dancers to show off their style. Songs include Trick songs, fast and slow Grass Dance songs, Shake songs, Crow Hops, Sneak Ups. Song structure consists of chorus and verses, some using real words and other vocables.

    Certain groups are known for their quality, and the dancers will honor these drum groups by whistling for them to repeat a song. Songs are passed on by oral tradition among groups with names such as Eagle Whistles, Haystack Ramblers, the Young Grey Horse Society.

Annual Powwow Events
▼▼▼▼▼▼▼▼

Most powwows stay within a certain week or weekend each year. This listing is not an exhaustive one, and dates are subject to change.

JANUARY
2nd weekend
Ermineskin Inauguration
Powwow
Hobbema, Alberta
Canada
(403) 585-3941

Indian Ceremonial
Show & Powwow
Santa Monica, CA
(213) 430-5112

Colorado Indian Art
Market
Denver, CO
(303) 447-9967

FEBRUARY
2nd weekend
Seminole Tribal Fair &
Rodeo
Hollywood, FL
(305) 321-1051

Lincoln's Birthday & Self
Government
Sovereignty Celebration
Warm Springs, OR
(503) 553-3393

3rd weekend
Washington's Birthday
Celebration
Toppenish, WA
(509) 865-5121

MARCH
1st weekend
Heard Museum Indian
Fair
Phoenix, AZ
(602) 252-8840

Powwow
Portland, OR
(503) 657-2510

Great Lakes Indian
Cultural Assoc.
Powwow
Ososso, MI
(313) 498-3449

2nd weekend
E-Peh-Tes Powwow
Lapwai, ID
(208) 843-2253

Spring Powwow
Cass Lake, MN
(218) 335-6211

4th weekend
Denver March Powwow
Denver, CO
(303) 936-4826

Scottsdale All Indian
Powwow
Scottsdale, AZ
(602) 569-0728

APRIL
1st weekend
Blacklodge Celebration
White Swan, WA
(509) 865-5121

Annual Spring Powwow
Laramie, WY
(307) 766-6189

Powwow
San Jose, CA
(408) 971-9631

Annual Oklahoma
Indian Education
Expo.
Norman, OK
(405) 325-4127

Annual Powwow
Tempe, AZ
(602) 784-3819

2nd weekend
All Indian Days
Powwow
Scottsdale, AZ
(602) 946-4228

3rd weekend
NASA Powwow
Cheney, WA
(509) 359-2441

Annual Powwow
Bellingham, WA
(206) 384-4849

Annual American
Indian Days
Chico, CA
(916) 895-6485

Tewaquachi Powwow
Fresno, CA
(209) 266-3477

Powwow & Art Mart
United Blackfoot Assoc.
& United Indians
Seattle, WA
(206) 329-5807

NASU Annual Powwow
Eugene, OR
(503) 737-2738

American Indian Week
Albuquerque, NM
(800) 288-0721

U.C. Berkeley Powwow
Berkeley, CA
(415) 642-6613

Bill Wahpepah
Powwow
Oakland, CA
(415) 531-6218

Annual South Umpaqua
Powwow
Myrtle Creek, OR
(503) 863-4942

4th weekend
Texas Gulf TIA-PIAH
Powwow
New Carey, TX
(713) 423-0583

University of Washing-
ton Powwow
Seattle, WA
(206) 543-9242

MAY
1st weekend
University of Montana
KYI-YO Powwow
Missoula, MT
(406) 243-5831

Southern Ute Tribal
Bear Dance
Ignacio, CO
(303) 563-4525

University of Nevada
Powwow
Reno, NV
(702) 359-7580

Montana State
University
Bozeman, MT
(406) 994-0211

Allard's Powwow &
Buffalo Feast
St. Ignatius, MT
(406) 745-2951

2nd weekend
Spring Powwow
Portland, OR
(503) 725-4452

Annual Intertribal
Powwow
Victoria, B.C. Canada
(604) 874-4231

Annual Powwow
Stanford University
Palo Alto, CA
(415) 725-6944

TSE-HO-Tso Intertribal
Powwow
Fort Defiance, AZ
(602) 729-5704

Bridging the Gap
Powwow
Calgary, Alberta
Canada
(403) 264-1155

Red Mountain Powwow
& Rodeo
Ft. McDermitt, NV
(702) 532-8259

Spring Powwow
Salem, OR
(503) 399-5721

Tuscarora Nation of
North Carolina
Powwow
Maxton, N.C.
(919) 844-3352

3rd weekend
Annual Montana Spring
Renaissance Festival
Eastern Montana
University
Billings, MT
(406) 657-2365

Annual Turtle Powwow
Niagara Falls, N.Y.
(718) 284-2427

NASA Powwow
Corvallis, OR
(503) 725-3723

Annual NASO
Powwow
Spokane, WA
(509) 536-8666

United Powwow
Omak, WA
(509) 826-2097

Mat 'Alyma Root
Festival
Kamiah, ID
(208) 935-2144

Cathedral Lake May
Day Celebration
Cathedral Lake, Alberta
Canada
(604) 499-5528

4th weekend
Chief Schonchin Days
Powwow
Klamath Falls, OR
(503) 783-2218

Red Nations Celebra-
tion
Long Beach, CA
(213) 738-2627

DE-Un-Da-Ga Powwow
Penn Run, PA
(412) 547-8442

Blackfeet Community
College Conference &
Powwow
Browning, MT
(406) 338-5441

Casa De Fruta
Memorial Day
Powwow
Hollister, CA
(408) 426-8211

Burnt Corn Rodeo &
Powwow
Pinon, AZ

Omaha Memorial Day
Celebration
Macy, NE
(402) 837-5391

Memorial Day weekend
Santa Fe Powwow &
Market
Santa Fe, NM
(505) 983-5220

Weaseltail Powwow
White Swan, WA
(509) 865-5121

Choctaw Annual Rodeo
Hartshorne, OK
(405) 924-8280

Kenel Powwow
Kenel, SD
(701) 854-7231

JUNE
1st weekend
Morton Powwow
Morton, MN
(507) 697-3250

2nd weekend
Sac & Fox All Indian
Pro Rodeo
Stroud, OK
(405) 273-0579

Tinowit International
Powwow
White Swan, WA
(509) 865-5121

First Peoples Powwow
Camp Rotary, MI
(313) 756-1350

Cannonball Annual
Weekend
Cannonball, ND
(701) 854-7231

Red Earth Native
American ultural
Festival
Oklahoma City, OK
(405) 232-2784

Native American Indian
Women's Conference
Lewiston, ID
(202) 546-9404

3rd weekend
Creek Nation Festival
Okmalgee, OK
(405) 756-8700

Annual Sam Yazzie Jr.
Memorial Powwow
Lukachukai, AZ
(602) 787-2301

Chief Joseph &
Warriors Memorial
Powwow
Lapwai, ID
(208) 843-2253

City of Roses Powwow
Portland, OR

Porcupine Powwow
Shields, ND
(701) 854-7231

Annual Prescott All
Indian Powwow
Prescott, AZ
(602) 445-8790

Annual Powwow &
Barbecue
Carson City, NV
(702) 882-1808

Red Bottom Celebration
Fraser, MT
(406) 477-6284

Shoshone Indian Days
Fort Washakie, WA
(307) 255-8265

Indian Hill Powwow
Tehachapi, CA
(805) 822-6613

PI-Um-Sha Powwow &
Treaty Days
Warm Springs, OR
(503) 553-1161

Father's Day
weekend
Community Powwow
Arapahoe, WY
(307) 856-6117

4th weekend
Badlands Celebration
Brockton, MT
(406) 768-5151

Last weekend
Saddle Lake Indian
Days
Saddle Lake, Alberta
Canada
(403) 726-3829

Annual Pawnee Indian
Homecoming &
Powwow
Pawnee, OK
(918) 762-3962

Coquille Indian Tribe
Powwow
Bandon, OR
(503) 888-4274

JULY
1st week
4th of July Powwow &
Open Rodeo
Nespelem, WA
(509) 634-4711

Annual Northern
Cheyenne Powwow
Lame Deer, MT
(406) 477-6284

Arlee Powwow &
Celebration
Arlee, MT
(406) 745-4242

Sisseton-Wahpeton
Powwow
Sisseton, SD
(605) 698-7676

**4th of July week-
end**
Tonto Apache July 4th
Celebration
Payson, AZ
(602) 474-5000

July 4th Celebration
Oraibi, AZ
(602) 734-2441

Indian Days Encamp-
ment & Powwow
White Swan, WA
(509) 865-5121

Shoshone-Paiute Annual
Powwow
Owyhee, NV
(702) 757-3161

Fort Kipp Celebration
Fort Kipp, MT
(406) 786-3369

Wakpamni Lake
Powwow
Batesland, SD
(605) 867-5821

July 4th Celebration
Powwow & Rodeo
Window Rock, AZ
(602) 871-6645

Chief Taholah Days
Taholah, WA
(206) 276-8211

Leech Lake Powwow
Cass Lake, MN
(218) 335-6211

Annual Chumash
Intertribal Powwow
Santa Ynez, CA
(805) 686-1416

1st weekend
Annual Northern Ute
Powwow & Rodeo
Fort Duchesne, UT
(801) 722-5141

Poundmaker-Nechi
Powwow
St. Albert, Alberta
Canada
(403) 458-1884

Bear Soldier Powwow
MacLaughlin, SD
(701) 854-7231

*Weekend after 4th
of July*
Black Hills & Northern
Plains Exposition
Rapid City, SD
(605) 341-0925

2nd weekend
Mission International
Powwow
Mission, B.C. Canada
(604) 826-1281

Calgary Stampede
Calgary, Alberta
Canada
(403) 261-0101

Little Hoop Traditional
Powwow
Mission, SD
(605) 747-2342

Hays Powwow
Hays, MT
(406) 358-2205

North American Indian
Days
Browning, MT

Arikara Celebration &
Powwow
White Shield, ND
(701) 627-4781

Annual Taos Pueblo
Powwow
Taos, NM
(800) 732-TAOS

Goodfish Lake Treaty
Celebration
Goodfish Lake, Alberta
Canada
(403) 636-3622

3rd weekend
Onion Lake Powwow
Saskatchewan—Alberta
Canada
(306) 344-2107

Antelope Powwow
Mission, SD
(605) 856-4713

Standing Arrow
Powwow
Elmo, MT
(406) 849-5541

Iron Ring Celebration
Poplar, MT

Mandaree Celebration
& Powwow
Mandaree, ND
(701) 627-4781

All Indian Stampede &
Pioneer Days
Fallon, NV
(702) 423-2544

Flandreau Santee Sioux
Powwow
Flandreau, SD
(605) 997-3891

Blood Indian Days
Standoff, Alberta
Canada
(403) 737-3753

Kickapoo Tribe in
Kansas Annual
Powwow
Horton, KS
(913) 486-2131

Ethete Powwow
Ethete, WY

Annual Powwow & Tipi
Village
Fort MacLeod, Alberta
Canada

Cheyenne Frontier Days
Cheyenne, WY
(800) 227-6336

4th weekend
Yukon Indian Days
Yukon Territory,
Canada
(403) 667-7631

Milk's Camp Traditional
Powwow
St. Charles—Bonesteel,
SD

Annual Traditional
Powwow
Corn Creek, SD
(605) 462-6281

Last weekend
Annual Chief Joseph
Days
Joseph, OR
(503) 432-1015

Annual Homecoming
Celebration
Winnebago, NE
(402) 878-2272

Sarcee Powwow &
Rodeo
Calgary, Alberta
Canada
(403) 281-9722

Little Eagle Annual
Powwow
Little Eagle, SD
(701) 854-3431

Fort Totten Annual
Wacipi
Fort Totten, ND
(701) 766-4221

Coeur d'Alene Powwow
Worley, ID
(208) 274-3101

Sweetgrass Band
Powwow
Saskatchewan Canada
(306) 937-2990

Milk River Indian Days
Fort Belknap, MT
(406) 353-2205

AUGUST
1st weekend
Northern Arapaho
Powwow
Arapaho, WY

Fort Randall Annual
Powwow
Lake Andes, SD
(605) 384-3804

Annual Indian Fair Days
& Powwow
Sierra Mono, CA
(209) 877-2115

Oglala Nation Fair &
Rodeo
Pine Ridge, SD
(605) 867-5821

Rocky Boy's Annual
Powwow
Rocky Boy's Agency, MT
(406) 395-4291

Standing Rock Annual
Powwow
Fort Yates, ND
(701) 854-3431

Annual Piegan Indian
Days
Brocket, Alberta
Canada
(403) 965-3939

2nd weekend
United Peoples
Powwow & Cultural
Rendezvous
Missoula, MT
(406) 728-2180

Bullhead Annual
Powwow
Bullhead, SD
(701) 854-7231

Lower Brule Annual
Powwow
Lower Brule, SD
(605) 473-5316

Ermineskin Indian Days
Hobbema, Alberta
Canada
(403) 585-3741

Omak Stampede,
Encampment & Rodeo
Omak, WA
(800) 572-6600

Little Shell Powwow
Newton, ND
(701) 627-4781

Parmelee Traditional
Powwow
Parmelee, SD
(605) 747-2136

Shoshone Bannock
Festival & Rodeo
Fort Hall, ID
(208) 238-3700

2nd week
Annual Intertribal Indian
Ceremonial
Gallup, NM
(800) 233-4528

3rd weekend
Chief Looking Glass
Powwow
Kamiah, ID
(208) 935-2144

Annual Chief Seattle
Days
Suquamish, WA
(206) 598-3311

Klamath Treaty Days
Powwow & Barbecue
Chiloquin, OR
(503) 783-2005

Kamloops Powwow
Kamloops, B.C.
Canada
(604) 372-9575

Twin Buttes Celebration
& Powwow
Twin Buttes, ND
(701) 627-4781

Crow Creek Annual
Powwow
Fort Thompson, SD
(605) 245-2221

White River Powwow
White River, SD
(605) 259-3670

Kalispel Powwow
Usk, WA
(509) 445-1147

Crow Fair & Rodeo
Crow Agency, MT
(406) 638-2601

Wakpala Powwow
Wakpala, SD
(701) 854-7231

Annual Rosebud Fair &
Powwow
Rosebud, SD
(605) 747-2381

Annual Southern
California Indian
Center Powwow
Costa Mesa, CA
(714) 530-0221

4th weekend
Oil Discovery Celebra-
tion Powwow
Poplar, MT
(406) 448-2546

SEPTEMBER
**Labor Day week-
end**
Cherokee Nation
Powwow
Tahlequah, OK
(918) 456-0671

Cheyenne & Arapaho
Labor Day Powwow
Colony, OK
(405) 323-3542

Wee-Gitchie-Ne-Me-E-
Dim Powwow
Cass Lake, MN
(218) 335-6211

Puyallup Tribe's Annual
Powwow & Salmon
Bake
(206) 597-6200

Annual Spokane Tribal
Fair & Powwow
Wellpinit, WA
(509) 258-4581

Awokpamani Omaha
Traditional Powwow
Poplar, MT
(406) 768-5155

Labor Day Powwow
Ethete, WY
(307) 856-6117

Annual Turtle Mountain
Powwow
Belcourt, ND
(701) 477-6451

Red Star Powwow
Reno, NV
(702) 329-2936

Cheyenne River Labor
Day Powwow
Eagle Butte, SD
(605) 964-4155

Shoshone Indian Fair
Fort Washakie, WY
(307) 323-9423

Annual Nakota
Powwow
Morley, Alberta
Canada
(403) 881-3939

Choctaw Nation Labor
Day Festival
Clayton, OK
(405) 924-8280

Potawatomi Powwow
South Bend, IN

Labor Day Weekend
Powwow
Binger, OK
(405) 656-2344

Bull Creek Traditional
Powwow
Dixon, SD
(605) 747-2381

Navajo Nation Fair
Window Rock, AZ
(602) 871-6659

1st weekend
Trail of Tears Intertribal
Powwow
Hopkinsville, KY
(502) 886-8033

Annual Blackhawk
Powwow
Pendleton, OR
(503) 276-3165

**1st weekend after
Labor Day**
Annual United Tribes
International Powwow
Bismark, ND
(701) 255-3285

Annual National
Championship
Powwow
Grand Prairie, TX
(214) 647-2331

2nd weekend
Southern Ute Tribal Fair
& Powwow
Ignacio, CO
(303) 563-4525

Pendleton Round-up
Pendleton, OR
(800) 524-2984

3rd weekend
Pine Nut Festival
Schurz, NV
(702) 773-2306

Choctaw Annual
Powwow
Canadian, OK
(405) 924-8280

Eagle Plume Society
Powwow
Nespelem, WA
(509) 634-4711

Helena Indian Alliance
and MUIA Powwow
Helena, MT
(406) 443-5350

Last weekend
National Indian Days
Parker, AZ
(602) 669-9211

OCTOBER
1st weekend
Cherokees of Georgia
Gathering Powwow
St. George, GA
(912) 843-2249

Annual Canadian
Thanksgiving
Powwow
Mt. Currie, B.C.
Canada
(604) 894-6867

3rd weekend
Powwow & Fall Festival
Native American Indian
Assoc. of Tennessee
Nashville, TN
(615) 726-0806

Apache Days
Globe, AZ
(602) 425-4495

Last weekend
Four Nations Powwow
Lapwai, ID
(208) 843-2253

NOVEMBER
Veterans Day
Veterans Day Powwow
Owyhee, NV
(702) 757-3161

Veterans Day Powwow
Salem, OR
(503) 399-5721

**Veterans Day
weekend**
Veterans Day Celebra-
tion
Toppenish, WA
(509) 865-5121

Veterans Day Powwow
Nespelem, WA
(509) 634-4711

Annual Veterans Day
Rodeo & Fair
San Carlos Apache
Reservation, AZ
(602) 475-2361

Veterans Memorial
Powwow
Oraibi, AZ
(602) 734-2441 ext
215

Annual Veterans
Powwow
Hobbema, Alberta
Canada
(403) 585-3739

**Thanksgiving
weekend**
Annual Powwow
Fort Duchesne, UT
(801) 722-5141

December
Many reservations hold
Christmas and New
Year's holiday
powwows.